GOD'S
SPIRITUAL
HOUSE

A Classic Study
on the Ministry
of Jesus Christ
in the Church

T. AUSTIN SPARKS

GOD'S SPIRITUAL HOUSE

A Classic Study
on the Ministry
of Jesus Christ
in the Church

Published by MercyPlace Ministries

MercyPlace is a licensed imprint of Destiny Image₀, Inc.

Distributed by

Destiny Image₀ Publishers, Inc.
P.O. Box 310
Shippensburg, PA 17257-0310

ISBN 0-9707919-0-9

For Worldwide Distribution
Printed in the U.S.A.

This book and all other Destiny Image, Revival Press, MercyPlace, Fresh Bread, Destiny Image Fiction, and Treasure House books are available at Christian bookstores and distributors worldwide.

For a U.S. bookstore nearest you, call **1-800-722-6774**.
For more information on foreign distributors, call **717-532-3040**.
Or reach us on the Internet: **www.destinyimage.com**

CONTENTS

FOREWORD

MEET T. AUSTIN SPARKS

T. Austin Sparks was one of those luminaries who brightened the years 1930-1970...years that were spiritually dry, both in the United States and Great Britain.

Church historians, as they record past history, look for men who are called *dissenters*, that is, the men who emerge outside the institutional church in every century. Consistently, historians have noted that these men were truly great contributors of new things during the centuries in which they lived. T. Austin Sparks was one of those men, and he was a giant among giants.

In the twentieth century the men whose names have emerged so far as being part of that rare breed are Watchman Nee of China, Prem Predham of Nepal, Bakht Singh of India, and T. Austin Sparks of Great Britain. They stood unequivocally as one voice outside the institutional church. Of the four, only Nee and Sparks wrote extensively. Watchman Nee's books number about 200. T. Austin Sparks's books number over 100. Their writings give us a rare insight into the minds of men who think and live outside the mind-set of the traditional church. Interestingly enough, the two men were friends, contemporaries, and one another's mentors.

Much is known of Watchman Nee, and virtually his entire ministry on this earth can be found in books. This preservation of Nee's spoken ministry can be attributed to the fact that Nee was the founder of a church movement in Asia, referred to as "The Little Flock." On the other hand, T. Austin Sparks raised up only one work, "The New Christian Fellowship," located on a street called Honor Oak. His ministry is often referred to as "The Honor Oak Ministry."

It is interesting to note that God raised up these men to speak to the first half of the twentieth century. Watchman Nee was born around 1900. His spoken ministry ended in 1950. T. Austin Sparks was born in 1888. Bakht Singh was also born at the beginning of the twentieth century. History waits to discover whom God raised up to speak to the last half of the twentieth century...and those men who will speak to the twenty-first century.

Now it is time for Christians to discover T. Austin Sparks. There is something high and unique, as well as an imcomparable depth, about this man's ministry. There simply isn't anything in other ministries that is so clearly focused on the centrality of Christ. What he gives us cannot be laid hold of in any other place.

In many ways it could be said that T. Austin Sparks had the deepest and richest ministry released in English by any man outside the institutional church.

To miss the ministry of T. Austin Sparks is to miss one of the great contributions made to the Christian family in modern times. Read him, and read him well.

—Gene Edwards
America's Best Loved Story Teller

CHAPTER ONE

THE EXALTATION OF GOD'S SON

Reading: 2 Chronicles 22:1-19; 28:5-7; 29:20,22-25;
Acts 2:30-36; 7:47-49; 2 Peter 2:4-5;
Hebrews 3:6; 12:5,9; Ephesians 1:20-23.

I have been very much occupied of late with this matter of sonship in the House of God, and am led to the conclusion that something of this is to be the Lord's message at this time. There are many aspects of this spiritual house. How many of them we shall be able to consider must remain to be seen.

It is quite certain that this matter is very relevant to what is happening at this present time on the earth. In particular, there is a very real and living message in it for the Lord's people, and I trust that we shall seek to adjust ourselves to that fact and not regard this as just some further measure of Bible teaching which may be more or less familiar.

CHRIST EXALTED ON HIGH—
THE KEYSTONE OF TESTIMONY

We shall begin with what the Scriptures so clearly indicate as the point of commencement of the House of God, namely, the exaltation of the Son to the place of supreme authority and glory. The spiritual house (which house are we) prospectively exists for this very purpose of proclaiming and rejoicing in the fact of the exaltation of God's Son. The passages we read from the Old Testament, which are prophetic, pointing on to the spiritual house, all bear out this fact and show it in type in a very wonderful and clear way. David's greatest son—for God had given him many sons—was brought out into clear view as the one chosen of God to be exalted to a place of glory and power above that which had been given to any before him; and it is interesting to note that, while Solomon was ordained and chosen of God for that position, he did not come out as distinguished for it until someone else made a bid for that position. You will remember the little incident of Adonijah, who subtly worked to get the throne, to get what God had appointed for Solomon. By that subtle movement to usurp the throne appointed for another, Solomon was distinguished at once, brought out and proclaimed as the one chosen by God. That is only in passing; but it is interesting to notice that it was when God's Son and God's appointment concerning His Son was assailed, and His place sought after in a conspiracy, that the Lord Jesus was marked out, brought out into the light as the One whom God had chosen. That is something which recurs. There it was in the case of Solomon. It was so in the case of the Lord Jesus at the beginning of this dispensation. That will happen again at the end when Antichrist makes his bid for world domination, and then God will bring out His Son as the One chosen and anointed for that position, and all will submitting to Him. It is the way of blessing. You see, all the blessing that God meant for man, the fulness that was to be man's inheritance, was lost because Satan, seeking to usurp the place of God's Son as Lord, by his propaganda worked subtly and made man believe that he would lose everything by remaining in subjection to God. "Why not be as God yourself?" said he. In other words, Why have a life limited by being subject to God and dependent upon Him! Along that line, man lost all the fulness, and now all the fulness comes back by being absolutely subject to God's Son, and submitting to Him in all things. That was the great lie of Satan, and this is why Satan does not like Jesus Christ being Lord, and why he so strongly contends against any ministry that has in view that object, of bringing the Lord Jesus into His rightful place as supreme Lord in God's house. It is because by that his lie is exposed and the work which he achieved through his lie undone.

The whole question is that of the universal Lordship of Jesus Christ, and it is that which is coming out to-day as never before in the history of this world as the supreme issue. Who is going to be Lord in God's universe? Who is going to have world dominion? The enemy is still seeking to reach that end through man along the line of the lie, and we have never before known of his method being so tremendously, so universally and so insidiously employed—the lie! So much so, that for months past, this world has rocked on this question. Who can be trusted? Who can be believed? Who is speaking the truth? What man can you have confidence in? There has spread over the earth such an atmosphere of discrediting by lies that men almost look at those of their own household and wonder whether they can be trusted. That is a terrible reality in many lands. They dare not open their lips within the most limited circle, because truth faileth, trust-worthiness has been smitten

5

almost to the ground. The lie, the propaganda of lies; and all, mark you, with this one end in view, namely, to get a grip on the dominion of this world. That is Satan's work behind what we see going on, and when Jesus Christ comes into His place as absolute Lord in you and in me, something results which declares that Satan has been defeated; the lie is exposed.

The truth is that subjection to Jesus Christ is not a miserable life as a vassal. It is a life of triumph, a life of victory, a life of glory, a life of fulness. It is the blinding work of the enemy with men, to make them think that to belong to the Lord, to have the Lord in their lives, means they are going to lose all that is worthwhile, and be shut down, and all the time be poor cringing creatures, hardly able to lift their heads up, going about as beggars. That is Satan's lie. The Old Testament brings it out here so clearly that, when all things were subject to, submitting themselves to, God's appointed king, it was a time of fulness such as the people had never known; and so it is when Jesus is Lord within as in Heaven.

In those days, following that great day of Pentecost, the Church knew something of liberation, enlargement, enrichment, glory, power and fulness, and it all sprang from the fact that Jesus was Lord. They lived upon that ground and in the appreciation of that great fact. Life commenced there, testimony commenced there and commences there, and all our service for the Lord should spring out of this. There is no true service that does not spring out from this fact of the Lordship of Jesus Christ. You see, every revival or great spiritual renewal has been by the Lord coming back into His place. Go again over the Old Testament, and you have instance after instance when the Lord was brought back into His place—it was a wonderful time. Think, for instance, of the days of Hezekiah, of Josiah, when the Lord was given His place anew in a wonderful way. They came back to re-enthrone the Lord as Lord in their midst in an utter and full way, and they were great days. If you pass your eye over history, you see that all real spiritual awakenings—call them revivals or renewals—have circled round this one thing, that the Lord was brought back into His place. He was given His place as absolute Lord, and people went down before Him. That was the secret of it, and it is like that.

What is true in history, true in the wider way, is true in the individual life. So much of our trouble, our declension, our spiritual weakness and failure, is because He is not Lord. We are thankful to know Him as Saviour, we believe that He is in Heaven glorified, but there is a good deal of controversy within us on points. It all amounts to this one issue, namely, the utterness of His Lordship within, and, when those matters and controversies are settled, we find a new uprising of life. You can always have a little revival in your own heart on any one point where the Lord has a controversy with you. Test it. It may be only one point, but you know that one thing is holding you up. You have to get clear on that one thing, and when at last you go down with that thing under the Lord and put it under His feet, you have a little revival in your own heart and you come out with new life, new testimony, new release. Spread that over all things, and the kingdom has come. It is just like that.

THE CROSS AND THE LORDSHIP OF CHRIST

Well, this, His spiritual house, has been brought into being for no other purpose or no greater purpose than that—just to stand entirely in the enjoyment of the proclamation of the exaltation of the Lord Jesus. When you come to think of it, is not that the primary and deepest meaning and purpose of the Cross? The Cross may do many things, touch many questions and many issues, but when you get down to the meaning of the Cross at its deepest, it relates to the deposing of other gods. That was the great issue in the twenty-fourth chapter of Joshua, you remember. In reviewing the whole situation, Joshua has all Israel before him, and he begins with the history of Israel right back in the time of Abraham's father. "Abraham's father lived in Ur of the Chaldees and served other gods. Then Abraham came out from the serving of his father's gods and crossed over the river and came into the land. After this your fathers came into Egypt and there they worshipped the gods of the Egyptians; but at length they also came out over the river to serve the Lord." The whole issue was other gods and the river between the other gods and the Lord every time.

Now then, what about you? says Joshua. Are you going to allow the river really to stand effectively for what it means? Are you going to allow that river really to stand between you and the other gods which you worshipped and served in Egypt? "As for me and my house, we will serve the Lord." What about you? So the river was always related to other gods. The Cross, in its deepest meaning, touches other gods, other lords, other objects of worship receiving the good of our lives, and deposes them all, and brings the Lord into His place, so that we say, "As for me and my house, we will serve the Lord." That is the meaning of the Cross. It touches everything that stands in the way of the absolute Lordship of Jesus Christ. It gets right down there.

8

THE LORD JESUS EXALTED AS OUR KINSMAN

By then there is this other or further very blessed fact about the exaltation of the Lord Jesus. He is exalted as our Kinsman. The exaltation of Christ is the exaltation of our Brother. That comes out, you see, in the record. David said, "Of all my sons (for Jehovah hath given me many sons), he hath chosen Solomon my son to sit upon the throne of the kingdom of Jehovah over Israel" (1 Chronicles 28:5, A.S.V.). Then later, when speaking of Solomon's enthronement, the record says, And all the sons of David bowed down and did obeisance to Solomon and submitted themselves unto him. A great thing— his brethren all looking up to him as on the throne and acknowledging him as king. This is a permanent factor in all the types about the exaltation of the Lord Jesus.

In the Book of Samuel, again, you have that time when Absalom had usurped the throne and brought a great deal of misery and suffering upon the people to whom he had promised so much; and then Absalom was slain and the people were stranded. For some time everything was in a state of suspense, until there arose a questioning among the people, and someone said, "Why speak ye not a word of bringing the king back?" That became a rumour, and it got out over to where David was. David heard what was being said, and he took hold of it and sent a message to Zadok and Abiathar for the people, expressing himself thus: I am your flesh and your bone; ye are my brethren; why speak ye not a word of bringing the king back? His appeal for his place was on the basis of his kinship and they brought him back on the basis of that appeal.

Now, what is the meaning and value of that? Well, God has exalted our Brother, God has exalted our Kinsman, and that

Kinsman is God's Son, and He, as the Apostle puts it, is going to bring many sons to glory because He is the first-born among many brethren. The exaltation of our Kinsman means that the family is coming to exaltation. His enthronement is the earnest of ours; and, beloved, we are never sure of coming to our exaltation, our fulness, until we recognize the Lord Jesus in His place as our Kinsman-representative. It is an exalted family, it is a household, you see; God's house for the Son, and then sons. But the Son must have His place before the sons can have theirs; but, having His place, the sons have theirs guaranteed to them. Our Kinsman is exalted, and that says a great deal; because He is not exalted just as a despot, just as an officially appointed monarch whether we like it or not—God has chosen Him, selected Him, put Him in that position; now then, Bow the knee! Oh no; He is our Brother, our Kinsman, and there is such a tie, such a link, such a oneness of life, that He cannot be there apart from us. There is an inward spiritual oneness with Him in His exaltation which spells something very big.

Perhaps I can illustrate it best by reminding you of Mordecai. You remember Haman again, in the train of these many usurpers, and Haman's devilish device to destroy all the Jews. Mordecai is in the place of rejection, ruled out. Then, by one of those marvellous acts of Divine sovereignty which make even a sleepless night of the most tremendous value in history, the king could not sleep one night. Would that all our sleepless nights were as profitable to the Lord as his was! He commanded to bring the book of records of the chronicles, and they were read before the king; and he read something about Mordecai. Someone had lifted up his hand against the throne and a certain man, a Jew, had brought the thing to light and saved the king's life. Then the king said, "What honour and dignity hath been done to Mordecai for this?" Then the story develops and it comes to the point where Haman goes home one day to his wife and all his friends and tells them of what had happened. He, who thought the king was going to honour him, has been made to honour Mordecai, and as he tells them this, the discerning answer made to Haman was this: "If Mordecai be of the seed of the Jews, before whom thou hast begun to fall, thou shalt not prevail against him, but shalt surely fall before him." If he is of the seed of the Jews, you cannot prevail, your days are numbered! There is something about that, you see. It is this kinship with the Jews on the part of the exalted one which secures both their deliverance and the enemy's undoing.

Oh yes, this kinship with the Exalted One means for us deliverance and the overthrow of the enemy. There is a very great deal bound up with the exaltation of the Lord Jesus, and Satan knows it. He knows that his days are numbered when Christ is exalted in any life. When we come to that exaltation-union with the Lord Jesus in our hearts, Satan is in despair. It is like that.

THE NEED FOR DILIGENCE AND DISCIPLINE IN THE LIGHT OF A DAY TO COME

Well now, we must stop somewhere, and I think we might just stay here by pointing out that this house, with all the significance of sonship, the Son and the sons in God's House, has a present spiritual meaning. It is something which has to be realized in a spiritual way now. It indeed is the great spiritual matter for all the children of God. If we ask, What is the issue in this dispensation where God and His people are concerned, the answer surely is this, that there shall be a house, a spiritual house, which stands in the good of the exaltation of the Lord Jesus. That is the issue, and that is to be a spiritual thing now.

But I also want you to remember that, so far as manifestation is concerned, this lies in the future; and upon that hangs this wonderful and terrible little word "if." "Christ as a son over [God's] house; whose house are we, if...." Hebrews 12, which treats of God's dealings with us as with sons, has a big "if" there also. "If ye endure chastening, God dealeth with you as with sons." It is rather a strange way of putting things. It almost looks as though you are not a son if you do not endure chastening. Well, that is what it means. The "if" is in view of the fact that you and I have not yet come to the fulness of sonship. It will be the fulness of sonship in manifestation which brings in the House of God in all its glory. It is something future, it is prospective. If...if...

You notice, in that connection, how Israel in the wilderness is so often called up as a warning. They did not become, in God's intended sense, His house. They have perished in the wilderness. They did not suffer chastening. They would not let God deal with them as with sons along the line of child-training. They did not come to their adoption as sons. They fell short of the glory of the inheritance of the full purpose of God; and that is brought over to Corinthians and to Hebrews as the warning. We are His house if...if...if...

Now, what is the significance of this? Oh, it is this, that what God's Son is in glory, He becomes in us now progressively; that Christ is being more and more enlarged in us as the Son over God's house. I think it is so patent, as hardly to need pointing out, that the course of our spiritual experience under the hand of God is always with this one thing in view. All our difficulties with the Lord, all our bad times, are on the principle of submission to the Lord, with a view to the Lord having His place. Is it not like that? The Lord is finding us out by child-training. Take up the child and put the child under training, and you will discover what is in the child, whether the child is going to be compliant or not, whether the child is going on with you or not. Put the child under discipline, and you will find out all the revolt that is in the child's nature. That is how the Lord is dealing with us.

The word "chastening" is unfortunate, because it is confused in our minds with punishing. It means nothing of the kind. God is not punishing His children at all. The true meaning is child-training, and Satan always turns God's dealings with us into punishment in our minds. It is not that. What He is working at with us is to bring us to the place where He is utterly Lord and can do as He likes with us, and we have no question at all. None of us has reached that point yet, but that is what the Lord is doing, and there is a big "if," you see. We can say we are not going to have any more of this discipline, we are not going on with it. Well, the throne is in view, not only for Him but for us. The Lord has a great purpose for His sons in union with the Son as joint-heirs and as fellow-rulers in His universe. It all springs out of the fact that Jesus Christ is Lord in Heaven and in us, and then that this Lordship is wrought into us in a perfect way. All our training is in that direction. So it is prospective, it is future, and the "if" is there. We are God's house if....May the Lord so triumph in us that the "if" greatly loses weight and power and place, and eventually ceases to be at all, and we are His house.

CHAPTER TWO

ASSURANCE AS TO GOD'S REST AND SATISFACTION IN CHRIST

...having foreordained us unto adoption as sons through Jesus Christ unto himself, according to the good pleasure of his will, to the praise of the glory of his grace, which he freely bestowed on us in the Beloved....to the end that we should be unto the praise of his glory, we who had before hoped in Christ (Ephesians 1: 5-6,12, A.S.V.).

For we are his workmanship, created in Christ Jesus for good works, which God afore prepared that we should walk in them (Ephesians 2:10, A.S.V.).

And now, O Father, glorify thou me with thine own self with the glory which I had with thee before the world was (John 17:5).

We are at this time being directed to take account of God's spiritual house, and in our previous meditation we were thinking of the first and preeminent feature of this spiritual house, in which we, in Christ, are living stones, as being the proclamation or setting forth of the exaltation of God's Son. We noticed that everything, so far as God's house is concerned, takes its rise from that exaltation. What happened on the day of Pentecost was the spontaneous outflow of that exaltation of God's Son to the right hand of the Majesty on high; and the secret of life, of power, of victory, in those first days of the Church's life and history was this very fact. Its life flowed out from this; its testimony was this, that Jesus as God's Son was exalted to the throne on high. You know that was the testimony of Peter on the day of Pentecost. You know that was the note of Stephen. You know the Apostles continually testified to that great fact, that God had made Him Lord and Christ, that He was exalted. I repeat, everything came out of that, and it resolves itself into the great element of assurance, something which is always very necessary; and never was there a time when it was more necessary than now.

THE ASSAULT UPON ASSURANCE

In our previous meditation, we referred to the fact that the great spiritual enemy has pursued his ambition for world dominion along the line of the propagation of a lie, his great "fifth column" propaganda, and he has made great headway by the campaign of lies to the undermining of assurance and confidence.

There is another thing which he has done and is doing in a spiritual way, which is so clearly seen at present working out along temporal lines, and is indeed the confessed and published strategy of those who are now being driven and used and governed by Satan toward world domination by the elimination of Christ. They have put it on record that their strategy is to work secretly within the national life of their enemies steadily through the years, with a view to bringing about internal disintegration by the breakdown of confidence; and how they have done it and are doing it! I do not want to dwell on the earthly, temporal and political side of things, but it does disclose the principles of Satanic activity, this working subtly and secretly behind the scenes within the life of their enemies with a view to destroying confidence, and so bringing about collapse from the inside. Indeed, the phrase which is in print in that connection is, We will make our enemies defeat themselves! Well, they have done it in many countries.

Now, take it as a clue to what is happening spiritually. Oh, how Satan has pursued that course right through history, to destroy confidence; for confidence is a tremendous factor. You see how nations seek to bolster up and stimulate assurance within their own borders in order to secure strength against their enemies. What will they not do to reassure people, to put confidence into people? Satan knows that an assured people set him the biggest problem and represent the most impossible situation for him. Now, if you look at those first days of the Church's life, one outstanding feature was this assurance. They were men without questions, people without doubts. They could speak with authority because their hearts were settled; they were not divided inwardly. There were none of the seeds of internal disintegration. The basis of that assurance and settled position was just this, that the Holy Spirit had come and in them had mightily registered the fact that Jesus was on the throne. "Jesus...by the right hand of God exalted." They had no question about that, and therefore all doubts were set at rest. The exaltation of the Lord Jesus, when it becomes something settled in our own hearts, is a mighty factor in testimony, in life, in service, and unless we have it we are altogether at a discount.

Now, in days such as these in which we are living, the strategy of the enemy is to undermine assurance. I am not speaking about worldly things now, but spiritual assurance. The House of God is therefore built by this means, the assurance that Jesus Christ is exalted, and you cannot build without it. In the case of David and Solomon, we noted how the bringing in of that house for the Lord God which was to be exceeding magnificent, all sprang from the fact that God had secured both His king and the throne for His king. God made a covenant with David. God took an oath with David that of the fruit of his loins should one sit upon his throne, and his throne should be established for ever. Now, that is transferred, as you know, to the Lord Jesus. It only had a merely figurative and very imperfect fulfillment in Solomon. Solomon came to a shameful end, but in the days of his glory he was a figure of another. Thus in the Book of the Acts we have those words quoted from the Psalm:

> *The Lord said unto my Lord, Sit thou on my right*
> *hand, till I make thine enemies the footstool of thy*
> *feet* (Acts 2:34-35, A.S.V.).

The Apostle uses those words in connection with this other word to David: "David...being therefore a prophet, and knowing that God had sworn with an oath to him, that of the fruit of his loins he would set one upon his throne; he foreseeing this spake of...the Christ," spake of this One; and God has fulfilled His word, not in a shadow, not in a type, but right up to the hilt in this greater Son of David. David's greater Son is on the throne of thrones, and out of God's securing His King in glory and exaltation, the history of the Church begins, and the supreme note by which the Church is built is the note of absolute assurance which comes from what God has secured in glory in His Son.

GOD'S REST IN HIS SON

Assurance comes from heart rest. Here again let us mark and how full of truth, exactitude, the Scriptures are everywhere— that it was no accident or chance or hap that Solomon, the man who was chosen for this position, had the name of Solomon. Solomon means "rest." Now you notice Stephen, referring to Solomon, says a rather interesting thing in Acts 7:47-49, A.S.V.:

> But Solomon built him a house. Howbeit the Most High dwelleth not in houses made with hands; as saith the prophet, The heaven is my throne, and the earth the footstool of my feet: what manner of house will ye build Me? saith the Lord: or what is the place of My rest?

Then Solomon had another name—*Jedidiah*, "Beloved of God." That is what we read in Ephesians—"hath made us accepted in the Beloved." You see, the Lord Jesus takes up Solomon on both his names. He is God's rest, "the place of my rest"; and He is the Beloved of God, the Beloved of the Father. So that, in the very first place, God gets all that His heart is set upon, with regard to what His house is to be, in the Person of His Son, and it is out of this that the house corporately, of which we are parts, takes its rise. It is built upon that heart rest which God has in His Son.

Now, you and I have to come to the same place as God in regard to the Lord Jesus before we can really be an expression of His house. We are His spiritual house: "Whose house are we." But that does not mean that God just puts us together as bricks. He must have living stones, and that phrase "living stones" implies, as the context shows in First Peter 2:4-5, A.S.V., that it is by a living relation with the chief Corner Stone that the house is built: "unto whom coming, a living stone…ye also, as living stones, are built up a spiritual house." The parts are one with the Corner Stone, all of a piece, so far as their nature is concerned, one with Him in what He is. As the building, we have to take our character from that chief Corner Stone which God has chosen. "I lay in Zion a chief corner stone, elect, precious." God works to Him and from Him. You and I work to Him and from Him. But what is this that gives the House its character? It is God's full and perfect satisfaction in His Son which gives Him rest. God rested from all His works on the seventh day, and God beheld all things which He had made, and they were very good.

Now, carry that right through in this spiritual connection with God's house, and long, long after you hear this word: "that he might present it [the church] to himself a glorious church, not having spot, or wrinkle, or any such thing." That is only saying, It is very good! The thing which first of all satisfies God's heart is that His Son has answered to all that He has ever required in a spiritual and a moral way. That is God's rest, and the exaltation of the Lord Jesus is God's seal to the fact. God is satisfied, God is at rest. Thus it is that, as the Lord Jesus is just about to step out on that last bit of the journey which is to see Him crucified, He says, "Father, glorify thou me with thine own self with the glory which I had with thee before the world was" (John 17:5). Glorify thou Me! Yes, that is coming almost at once by the darkest part of the road. It is the way to the glory. This last step, the Cross, is the final stage and summing up of all that has been in the satisfaction of God's heart.

THE VALUE OF THE BLOOD OF JESUS

What I am coming to in all that I have said is this, that it is by His precious Blood that God's absolute rest in the Lord Jesus is secured. Oh, beloved, you and I need ever more and more to apprehend the supreme value of the Blood of Jesus! The value of the Blood of Jesus is the great factor at the end time. It is the supreme factor in heart rest, and heart rest is the only ground of victory; and therefore Satan is always seeking to rob the children of God of heart rest on spiritual matters. I am going to make this appeal to you all at this time, although something more will have to be said at some other time about it; but I do want to make this appeal to you, that we ought to be at the place where the matter of our relationship with God in acceptance, in peace, in rest, in fellowship, is an absolute thing now. We must not allow the other side of our spiritual experience to cross that dividing line and come into the realm of our assurance. I mean, there is that other side where the Lord is conforming us to the image of His Son. He has a great work on hand in us, and, as He takes it in hand, we discover as never before what a work it is. We discover ourselves, dis-cover the depths of iniquity that are to be found in our fallen nature. It becomes a terrible thing to us. But never allow that which comes to light by God's handling of us to cross over into that other place of our acceptance, our standing, our peace with God.

So many people fail to keep that line clearly defined and they accept all kinds of accusations from the enemy because the Lord is dealing with them in this way. They feel so bad, so worthless, so useless, so utterly impotent and evil, and suppose therefore that their relationship with the Lord is interrupted, and the Lord is not pleased with them, and all that sort of thing, and they lose their rest. I believe that is why a lot of people have turned strongly against the subjective side of God's working, because they have seen many Christians altogether break down in their assurance under it. You come to a place where you know the Lord has accepted you and that you have peace with God; your sins are forgiven, and you are blessedly at peace, enjoying the Lord. Well, you are there for a time, and then you come into touch with something that has to do with spiritual progress and fuller life in Christ, and all that is bound up with that. Now many, as soon as they begin to touch that, lose their old basic assurance and joy, and because of that, there are those who have turned, not only against simple salvation and rejoicing in the Lord as Saviour, but all that is beyond besides. They will not have anymore. They will not have what is subjective. That does not justify their position, but it does say that we have to be very careful about this matter; and we have to stand up to this thing. We have to take this position, and no doubt some of you have taken this position—Well, I know I am beginning to know something of the depths of evil in my own nature; I am coming to see what I never would have believed to be true of myself. I have never had worse times about myself, the hopelessness of myself, than I am having now. I am seeing more and more that in me, that is in my flesh, dwelleth no good thing! and soon, but...but that is the Lord's matter. That is for the Lord to deal with. I am not going to allow that to encroach upon my absolute acceptance with God, my basic standing before God. I am not going to allow all the problems of sanctification to come over and destroy the great assurance of justification!

You must be very careful to keep that line clearly defined, because, if I am not mistaken, that is just the work of the devil to destroy the power of the Church, and I believe that that is the heart of Revelation 12:11, A.S.V.—"They overcame him because of the blood of the Lamb"—and who is it they are overcoming? The accuser of the brethren. He is seeking to cast them down by accusation, and their answer to his accusation is the Blood of the Lamb. What is that? God satisfied, God at rest, and I at rest on the basis of the Blood. They overcame him and he is cast down. They are not cast down when they maintain their position there. The Blood is not something just for initial salvation; it is something for final triumph; it is the final thing. The value of the Blood is a tremendous thing to keep the Lord's people strong and assured, confident, and with the ringing note of authority; God's basis of satisfaction, the Blood of His Son making possible His exaltation.

Well, this is all to do with that necessary, indispensable element of assurance by which the Church is built. The spiritual house goes forward on that line. I believe that that is the secret of the remarkable progress at the beginning. "The Lord added to the church daily those who were being saved." The Church grew in a way in which it has never grown since, and the great factor in the building of the house then, in the growth of the Church, was that there was this note of absolute assurance and confidence. They were a people who had heart rest, and who knew that Jesus Christ was enthroned. For them that settled matters in their hearts between themselves and God. That is all going back to our previous meditation, but it leads us right on to this further thing which the passages we have read bring specially before us. It is that the spiritual house has its existence for the very purpose of answering to God's own desire, ministering to God's own pleasure and glory. There are these phrases in Ephesians: "That we should be to the praise of his glory"; "to the praise of the glory of his grace," should exist to satisfy God's heart, to minister to His glory, to His pleasure. In this way, the spiritual house is to be God's answer to all that has happened in history.

GOD'S NEW CREATION

In the first creation gathered up into the first Adam, we have seen God surveying His working and saying, It is very good! Then followed breakdown, chaos, ruin in the creation. Out of a ruined creation, God lifted a nation, and the greatest thing that was ever said of Israel, I think, is in that little phrase, "Israel my glory." What a thing to say! Israel My glory! And in the early days of Solomon, Israel was God's glory. Again come breakdown, failure, ruin. Finally we see God coming back again, coming back on Israel, coming back on creation with a new creation in Christ Jesus. Firstly, as to Christ Himself personally, and being able to say, as we have seen, "My beloved, in whom I am well pleased," I am fully satisfied. In other words, it is the new creation seen in Christ, and God saying, It is very good, I am well pleased.

But then there comes in the Church, the Church which is His Body, which is an extension of the new creation from Christ personal to Christ corporate, and the last thing in view about this Church is its coming down from heaven having the glory of God, or, to use the other words, "presented unto him a glorious church," or again, "when he shall come to be glorified in

his saints, and to be marvelled at in all them that believed"
(2 Thessalonians 1:10, A.S.V.).

That is the end. So that this is God's final answer. There is
not going to be another chaos and ruin in the creation. This is
God's last answer to all that has gone before of ruin and breakdown. It is the Church, this spiritual house, a new creation.

WHAT THE CHURCH IS

What, then, is this spiritual house? What is this Church? Let
us not have an objective mentality about this, thinking of it as
something somewhere outside of and apart from ourselves.
What is it? The answer is a very simple one. The spiritual
house of God is Christ Himself. Yes,
but not Christ personally alone, but
Christ in you, in me, the hope of
glory. Oh, it is just here that all the
mistakes have been made about the
Church, with such disastrous results.
The Church, the House of God, is
simply Christ Himself in undivided
oneness found in all those in whom
He really dwells. That is all. That is
the Church. Seek to root out of your
mentality any and every other idea of
the Church. It is not Christ divided into a thousand or a mil-
lion fragments amongst so many believers. It is still one Christ.
You and I are not the Church. It is Christ in you and in me that
is the Church. We still remain what we are outside of the
Church still on our natural ground, but it is the measure of
Christ in us that constitutes the Church, a spiritual Church, a
spiritual house, the one Christ by the one Spirit in all those in

> The Church, the
> House of God, is
> simply Christ Himself
> in undivided oneness
> found in all those in
> whom He really
> dwells.

whom He dwells. That is the Church. God has never seen in that Church, in that Temple, anything but His Son. He is the Temple of God and you and I can never belong to the Church save as Christ is in us. I know that is a simple thing to say, but if we would just fasten on that and see what that means; it is one of the great factors of unspeakably great power against the enemy, if only we would live on that basis, if only we would abide there.

There are two ways of approaching the matter, and I see again the great success of Satanic propaganda in this matter. I do not know what you older Christians think about it. We can only speak of what we have recognized in our lifetime, but we have lived long enough to recognize the course of things, and to me it does seem, and it more than seems, that, in the last few years, the last few decades, there has been a far greater development and growth of suspicion amongst Christians than there used to be, so that to-day it is almost impossible to speak anywhere without people wondering if you are quite sound. It is in the atmosphere. It seems to me that there is a constant alertness to scent something that is not quite sound, and anything that is of God is prejudiced by that attitude, that state of things. The real truth of God is not getting a chance because this suspicion has spread over all the world, among all Christians. Is this quite right? Is this quite sound? Is this quite true? What is the snag here? What is the error in this? It is like that. That is the positive line, that has become the positive line, and, beloved, I believe that this is one of the marks of this Satanic propaganda to bring about collapse from the inside, because it means that there is internal disintegration, there is no cohesion, the people of God are broken up into thousands of fragments by this very spirit and atmosphere of suspicion bringing about prejudice, and the Church cannot move together as a solid whole.

There are very few Christians indeed who can move a hundred percent together, as one, simply because of this. Satan brings it into the most intimate circles of Christian life and fellowship, all the time bringing up this horrible element of uncertainty, question. Yes, he has gotten to the inside, and he is bringing about internal disintegration and collapse in a very quiet way, but subtly working through the years, and he can win many bloodless battles along that line. He can take territory very easily along that line and hold it and gain his end of dominion.

Take another earthly expression of this spiritual background of things. Do you not see, beloved, that over there there is no room whatever for a second thought or a second mind? Anybody through the last seven years who has had another thought, another mind, a second idea, has been eliminated. You may not there have two minds. You have got to subjugate your mind to this other mind, this dominating mind. You must not have an opinion, you must not reason, you must not speak in any way that cuts across the prevailing mind, the mind of the dictator. There is no room for anything that is second. It is one. Satan knows the almost infinite value of oneness, and that is a secret of progress, of success; a ruthless, murderous elimination of every second voice, to have only one voice, one mind, one will, dominating all others. Dare you think otherwise? Dare you have a mind of your own? Well, have it, but make very sure that you never let it be known. That is the regime, and what power there is for the object in view!

Well now, that is an earthly expression of a spiritual system. Bring that into the realm of the Church. Why is the Church

paralysed, weakened, held up? Why can it not go forward terrible as an army with banners? Because there has been this dis-
integrating work secretly going on within its borders, so that
suspicion is the order of the day. I suggest to you that, for the
sake of the overthrow of the Satanic kingdom which is to be
brought about by and through the Church in union with its
Head, its Lord, in glory, for the sake of that and unto the end,
you and I should make the opposite our positive course. Let
us not be for ever suspiciously asking, what is wrong? What is
doubtful? What is unsafe here? but positively, What is there of
Christ in this? On that I fasten! What do I see or sense of the
Lord Jesus in this matter? With that I engage, I co-operate. Oh,
if we would only take that as our positive course, Satan would
soon be losing ground, the Church would soon be coming up
a glorious Church. One thing which characterised the Church
at its beginning was oneness. They spoke the same things,
they were all of one mind and one heart, and what ground the
enemy lost! But, as soon as the enemy began his secret "fifth
column" work of propagating internal doubts, suspicions, prejudices, he very soon brought the Church down out of that
realm of reigning life and scattered its power.

Oh, we must pray the Lord that the one Christ, the one Spirit,
shall be in the ascendant in us! We shall not be living either
upon the ground of what we are naturally—for we shall always
be affected by what we are naturally, but upon the ground of
what there is of Christ in one another; neither let us be
dwelling upon the ground of possible error, possible false
teaching, and possibility of it being there all the time and
almost looking for that more than anything else. Oh, we must
trust the Lord about this matter! I do believe, beloved, that the
safest way, the way of our protection from error, is to go on
with the Lord. Our position must be—I am going on with the

Lord where I find the Lord, and I am going to trust the Lord in the matter of error, and, as we walk with the Lord, we shall sense, without looking for it, where the error is, and we shall be warned by the Spirit, we shall know. We must move on the positive basis, that of the Lord Himself, and that is glory in the Church, when it is the Lord. "Christ in you, the hope of glory."

We know quite well, in simple ways, that this is true. We meet one another, we have never met before. We discover very quickly by our spiritual sense that we belong to the Lord, and then we have a very blessed time simply on that ground. We flow together because we are the Lord's, and, if only we stood there, we would go on having a blessed time, but presently we begin to discuss some doctrine and find we do not agree. All the glory goes out, the fellowship breaks down. Oh, the Lord hold us into Himself!

Now, I am saying this spiritual house is Christ, and all that is not Christ has got to be kept in its own place, and we have got to seek to remain on the basis of Christ as in us and as in one another, and this is the glory of God, that we should be to the glory of His grace. That is where it begins—His grace. It seems to me, it has seemed to me through the years, (I do not know whether I am right in doctrine now or not, it is a forgivable mistake if it is error), but it has seemed to me through the years very often, that the Lord Himself has taken pains to keep me on the basis of grace, and by that I mean He has so often let me know in experience that, but for His grace, I am a lost man in experience, not a doctrine, not as truth.

Oh, to-day, it would be a bad thing for me if it were not for the grace of God! Yes, to appeal even to-day to the Blood, to the grace of God, because of that precious Blood, to-day, after so many years of knowing the Lord! Yes, it is grace to-day, and it is that that brings glory to God, allowing us to know how base, how foul, we are, and letting us know that that makes no difference to Him because of the Blood. That is glory to God. I do not know what the deepest note in your heart is to-day, but that is the deepest note in my own heart after these years. Ah, it is the grace of God that is the glory of my heart, the glory of His grace. He is glorified by our recognition of His grace and our abiding on the basis of His grace. The glory is soon taken away from the Lord when we get on to any other ground; what we are and can do and what we are doing.

The Lord will very soon put a stake in our flesh when we begin to get exalted like that. He is being robbed of glory. He is glorified by our transfiguration, our conformity to the image of His Son. Paul says, "We...beholding as in a mirror the glory of the Lord, are transformed into the same image" (2 Corinthians 3:18, A.S.V.). The glory is connected with the change, transformed into the same image. He is glorified as we are changed into the image of His Son. He is glorified when our lives are becoming fruitful. "Herein is my Father glorified, that ye bear much fruit" (John 15:8). And the fruit, in the first place, is the fruit of the nature of the Lord Jesus, the fruit of the Spirit, love, joy, peace, longsuffering, kindness, goodness, faith, meekness, self-control. "Herein is my Father glorified." Fruit in service, of course, but fruit in life, and He is glorified by the endurance of the saints.

Ah, yes, let us lay this to heart as our final word. If only we recognised it. There is a great deal of glory brought to the Lord simply along the line of endurance. At times we can do no more. The only thing to do is to give up or to hold on; to let go, or to endure. Peter has a lot to say about that. "This is grace, if a man endure," and just to endure brings glory to God. It will be a great story, it will be one of the large and glorious volumes in the library of Heaven, the story of the endurance of the saints, how much glory it brought to God. Oh, the story will be a romance! How many people were influenced by it, how many unbelievers came to believe because of the endurance of some saint in the time of suffering! How many other saints were mightily supported as they saw the steadfast endurance of another under fiercest trial! How much the Lord got out of just sheer endurance! Yes, this is to the glory of God, if we endure. The Lord get glory in the Church by Christ Jesus unto all ages for ever and ever, and may we indeed be a house for His glory in these various ways.

CHAPTER THREE

MINISTERING TO THE DELIVERANCE AND LIFE OF THE ELECT

*Unto whom coming, a living stone, rejected indeed
of men, but with God elect, precious, ye also, as
living stones, are built up a spiritual house, to be a
holy priesthood, to offer up spiritual sacrifices,
acceptable to God through Jesus Christ*
(1 Peter 2:4-5, A.S.V.).

*But the priests the Levites, the sons of Zadok, that
kept the charge of my sanctuary when the children
of Israel went astray from me, they shall come near
to me to minister unto me; and they shall stand
before me to offer unto me the fat and the blood,
saith the Lord Jehovah: they shall enter into my
sanctuary, and they shall come near to my table,
to minister unto me, and they shall keep my
charge. And it shall be that, when they enter in at
the gates of the inner court, they shall be clothed
with linen garments; and no wool shall come upon
them, while they minister in the gates of the inner*

> *court, and within. They shall have linen tires upon*
> *their heads, and shall have linen breeches upon*
> *their loins; they shall not gird themselves with any-*
> *thing that causeth sweat*
> (Ezekiel 44:15-18, A.S.V.).

We have been seeking to see some of the major features of this spiritual house, remembering the words of the Apostle, "Christ as a son, over [God's] house; whose house are we" (Hebrews 3:6, A.S.V.). Those features which we have already contemplated are that this spiritual house has as its object, in the first place, the setting forth of the exaltation of the Lord Jesus; in the second place, to be the vehicle through which the glory and pleasure of God are ministered to.

THE PRESENCE OF A SPIRITUAL HOUSE
THE SIGNAL FOR SATANIC ANTAGONISM

Now for a little while we will dwell upon the third of those major features, which is that, in the purpose of God, this spiritual house is here to minister for the deliverance and life of the elect. We will not dwell very much upon that last word, "the elect." We need not be particularly taken up with it. It is the people of God who are in view; the Church which is foreknown, elect according to the foreknowledge of God the Father, chosen in Christ before the world was, and the spiritual house exists to minister for the deliverance, and to the life, of that people. This is the great vocation of the people of God, or a part of that great vocation. So great, so vital is it, that immediately upon the bringing in of the Church, all hell was moved from beneath against it. The very bringing in of the Church was the signal and the occasion for a mighty move on the part of the enemy, a move along many lines and by many means, two of which can be clearly discerned, and indeed are being forced upon our attention in these days, if we recognize the fact that behind all that is taking place on the earth at this time there is a spiritual system of things. That twofold move on the part of the enemy from the beginning has been, firstly, by subtle working on the inside to bring the Church to a collapse inwardly; and secondly to overwhelm it by sheer force. I think we need say no more by way of indicating the nature of things. That is indeed Satanic and a Satanic method.

The first indication in the Church's history that Satan was at work was by that secret, inward, subtle movement of the enemy through Ananias and Sapphira, and it was pronounced immediately to be Satanic. "Why hath Satan filled thine heart...." It was something right from the inside and a subtle movement of Satan to bring about internal collapse. But for the swift judgment of God upon that thing, it would have spread like a canker. It would have worked subtly until the Church was seething with that sort of thing. Then, not long after, the other form of Satanic activity became manifest, namely open, direct, aggressive force to try by direct means to crush and trample under foot this instrument of God which had been brought into being; and all that which has been pursued relentlessly and on an ever-growing scale down the ages is itself significant as to the greatness of the vocation of the Church. It is indicative that Satan recognizes the issue to be himself or the Church; these two cannot proceed together.

Let me say again that we are not without ample evidence that the present world happenings are not merely political and temporal, but are spiritual in their nature and essence, and, as even men of the world recognize and pronounce, they are Satanic in their background. If that is true, we may come to one conclusion, namely, that it is not just the suppression of certain peoples on the earth which is in view with Satan. It is to get at something within or among the peoples which is a menace to that world domination of Satan through his Antichrist. If that really came home to our hearts as it ought to, and as it may yet be brought home more forcibly by sheer force of circumstances, we should recognize that not only is our existence as the Church at stake, but that we are up against the great test, perhaps the final test, of whether we are fulfilling our heavenly calling.

THE ASSAULT OF SATAN AGAINST CHRIST IN HIS HOUSE

You see, the whole effort of Satan from the beginning has been to destroy the life of God's people here on the earth. Christ's life in the Church is the objective of Satan in this dispensation, and, inasmuch as the Church is called into relationship with the working out of God's eternal purpose—for the Church is not only called according to that purpose, but is the elect instrument for the working out of that purpose—that very fact must involve the manifestation of the most terrible power that this universe contains against God's purpose.

THE GREATNESS OF GOD'S CHRIST

What is God's purpose? Well, it has to do with the first thing with which we were occupied in relation to this House of God, namely, the exaltation of God's Son to the throne of the universe. That is God's purpose comprehensively, inclusively; and the Church is called in, not only to share that exaltation; but to be instrumental in the working out of that purpose.

If that be true, then, we repeat, that involves the manifestation of this terrible power of Satan; because the exaltation of
the Lord Jesus to the supreme place is not a mechanical nor
automatic thing. It is a spiritual thing, and it is accomplished
by spiritual power. That is why we are designated "living
stones." We are not just bricks being put together; we are part
and parcel of the very life of Christ and of God's purpose concerning Christ, and it is that life of His in a final, full manifestation in the Church which will be the display of the glory of
the Lord Jesus. The Lord Jesus cannot be manifested in glory
as supreme Lord in God's universe until the elect come
through to that place of absolute triumph over all the power
of death, and thus it is by the Church's triumph that the glory
of Christ is displayed. It becomes therefore a living matter, a
spiritual matter, and not just a cold, lifeless, mechanical thing.
We are in something very real. We are going to know that, to
reach God's end, the instrument by which that purpose is
worked out to its completion has to come up against the last
fragment and ounce of Satanic power. It involves the drawing
out of Satan's power to the full in order that God may display
how great His Christ is.

That is the principle which has run right through the Word
of God. You can see it standing out again and again in con-
spicuous instances, one of which is contained in the word
addressed to Pharaoh: For this purpose have I raised you up,
that I might display in you my power. Pharaoh therefore was
allowed very much liberty. When Pharaoh in the very first test
refused God, God could have come in and crushed him and
destroyed him out of hand, and that would have been the end
of Pharaoh. But God drew him on, drew him out, once, twice,
thrice, on to ten times, the full measure of Pharaoh's resource;
drew him out and all that was instigating him, in order that,

showing how much power there was against God, God could come in at last and show how much greater He was than the greatest that was against Him. It is only a foreshadowing, a type.

But, you see, it is not with mere Pharaohs or dictators that we have to do. We are up against the full power of Satan himself. I say the Church is up against that, and the Church, as being the instrument of reaching God's end and fulfillling or working out God's purpose, has therefore to be proved absolutely superior to Satan. Where the Lord gets His life into His people, the one certain thing which will happen to that people is that they will be instrumental in drawing out death against themselves. It is true. It is remarkable, is it not? You wonder why it is that, the more closely you walk with the Lord and the more you are set upon God's full thought, the more you seem to be drawing death upon yourself. One thing with which you are always in conflict is this death-working activity of Satan. That is a part of our vocation. We do not like the idea, we inwardly shrink, and all that is natural about us feels very bad at the thought; but we just have to put all that on one side and trust the Lord in facing facts. We have to face spiritual facts. Therefore we take note of this, that, if it is true that this spiritual House, this Church, this Body of Christ is in existence as the instrument by which God is going to fulfil His purpose concerning His Son, then that can only be as all Satan's power is drawn out and exhausted, to the end that, in that Church, the life whereby Jesus conquered death should be manifested as greater than all the power of death itself. You see, then, the steps. The first is that the presence of a spiritual House here is the signal for Satanic action. The second is that the whole effort of Satan is set against Christ's life in that House, that Church, that Body. The third is that the very working out of

God's purpose through the Church, the House, necessitates the drawing out of Satan's power and the Church's experience of something very terrible, in respect of what Satan's power is, all to one end, namely, the bringing out, not of the greatness of Satan's power, but the greatness of God's Christ. That is the goal.

THE COURSE OF THE CONFLICT

It is quite clear that, through history, Satan has had a Satanic succession of instruments on the earth. He started with Cain. "Cain was of the evil one," the Scripture says, "and slew his brother" (1 Jn. 3:12 A.S.V.). Right down through history as disclosed in the Old Testament, you have Satan's unholy succession of instruments. Again and again you come upon them. There they are lying in wait right to his hand for death purposes. There is Doeg the Edomite to hand, subtly to hand, watching for his advantage, with his eye upon God's king. There is Haman, the Agagite, scheming and planning for the death of all the Jews. So Satan has had his succession of instruments for the death of God's people right up to to-day. They are at work to-day and we know their names. But God has had His line of succession all the way through from Abel onward. Now these, every one of them, drew out the power of the adversary. Abel drew out the power of death through Cain. It seems as though he went down under it, but it is not so. In the long run we know otherwise, and he, being dead, yet speaketh. His testimony remains. Thus every one of these links in the chain of God's successors has drawn out the adversary to display his power, and then eventually, although in their lives here on the earth they may have gone down under that power, the triumph is with that life which was in them, with the Lord whom they served. That is how it is now.

We must be very careful of our deductions, and in one connection especially, namely, with regard to the fact that the Lord
gives the enemy a good deal of rope, and the enemy gains
many advantages and has a large measure of success. But,
remember, Satan's power and Satan's success are not in spite
of God but because of God. If you can draw that distinction,
you will be greatly helped. Satan's power is not in spite of
God, but because of God. God is allowing it. It is under the
sovereignty of God. God is simply drawing it out, extending it,
and when the cup of iniquity is full, then God will come in and
show how overwhelming He is. That is the end. Beware of
your deductions when you see evil having a great measure of
success. Understand what God is doing. He is not going to
show His power against the thing in its infancy. What power
of God would that be? No, God displays His power when a
thing is full grown.

Now, while I must not diverge and get on to another very
important aspect of what we are considering, I would here
point out a very startling fact with reference to the matter of
sonship. While sonship, which is full-grown manhood, is a
Divine end, and with sonship comes the manifestation of
glory, (that is, when things have become full, then glory is
manifested—"[waiting] for the manifestation of the sons of
God,") sonship is also a principle operating on the side of
Satan. The Lord Jesus said to those Jewish rulers, "Ye compass
sea and land to make one proselyte; and when he is become
so, ye make him twofold more a *son* of hell than yourselves"
(see Matthew 23:15). He chooses His word—full-grown
expression of hell. A terrible thing! But, you see, all that happens on that side under the sovereignty of God is bringing
things to maturity before judgment comes in. The sovereignty
of God requires that iniquity must come to the full, and its

coming to the full is not because God is impotent or unable to cope with the thing. It is not in spite of God but because of God; and God is going to answer the sum of Satan's power through the Church. Thus, in the end, it will be "unto him be the glory in the church and in Christ Jesus unto all ages for ever and ever" (Ephesians 3:21 A.S.V.).

THE CHURCH'S VOCATION

Now then, what is the vocation of the Church in relation to all this? We are here, as we said at the outset, for the purpose of ministering to the deliverance and life of the elect. The real ministry arises in a day like this. It is the ministry of intercession, priestly intercession: "a spiritual house, an holy priesthood, to offer up spiritual sacrifices." We are being launched into our vocation now perhaps as never before as we see the enemy coming out more fiercely and terribly against the life of Christ in the Church. We are here to stand in God for that life, and we have to be very careful in this matter that we are not put off our ministry by any subtle, secret working of the enemy. We cannot say too much about this secret internal activity, this propaganda of the spiritual powers to put the people of God out of action by breakdown and collapse from within, and it is in this very connection that we have those assurances and exhortations with regard to our access unto God. Let us remember that these comforting words about access, of being allowed even boldness to draw nigh, are not just for our own comfort and satisfaction.

It is this vocation that is in view, and I believe that is proved again by the action of the enemy. Is he not continually trying to get the people off their ministry of prayer by throwing some doubt upon their acceptance, their access, bringing them under accusation and raising up the sense of some kind of spiritual barrier between them and the Lord so that the very heart is taken out of prayer. "What is the good of praying? There is that and there is that and the other thing about me; my very state keeps me from prayer." Ah, yes, and if we act upon that accusation, on the one hand it is a sheer denial of the value of the Blood, setting it aside, which is what Satan wants, and on the other hand it is playing into his hands and giving him the advantage over the people of God. Remember, all interference with our prayer life is a strategic movement on the enemy's part to destroy our vocation and to gain the advantage over the people of God. We are here for the deliverance and life of God's people. This is the very purpose of the Church's existence.

Now, will you take that as more than something just said? Will you listen to that from within? If you truly are a child of God, will you pray at this time that you may both see and accept all the meaning of the fact that you are a part of Christ's Body, a living stone in the spiritual house, and that your very existence as such is in relation to the life and deliverance of God's people everywhere. You are not an individual, you are a part of a house, and that house is God's means of deliverance and life for His people everywhere in this intensifying conflict with the power of death and darkness. We exist for that, and if we are not ministering to that, we are denying the very object of our existence. Do take that to heart, because there is no option about this. It is not an optional matter whether we fulfil an intercessory ministry or not, and pray for all saints at all seasons. You are not invited to come and do that *if you like*. That is not the House of God. We have to see that the House of God is not some inanimate lifeless thing. It is living, and the very marks of its life are that it is active, energetic, in a spiritual way; and it is characterised by the spirit of intercession. The position is not that you have prayer meetings at different times and people pray or do not pray according as they feel like it. The House is characterised by intercession, and it is that which determines whether we are corresponding to the very nature of our life as God's children. If we were really living up to what we are in Christ, whenever there is an opportunity to pray, we would be on the mark. At the least we should be alive to it, and, whether we prayed audibly or not, we would be in it; it would be spontaneous. Life is spontaneous; and so intercession is a part of life, which is spontaneous. If the Spirit of the Lord really has His way in us, we will be people of intercession. We cannot help it, it will be so.

But unto that, we have to watch these points where our intercession is assailed, and the points at which intercession or prayer is assailed are numerous. Remember, a basic point is this matter of access. We have to be sure of our access unto God, and to be sure about it, we have to know the infinite value of that precious Blood, and we must not be deterred by anything, for the Blood forbids us to be deterred. That Blood exists to deal with anything that would deter us. Yes, we may fail, we may blunder, we may break down; there may be those things which grieve us and grieve the Lord, but oh, let us recognize that the precious Blood makes possible the keeping of the shortest accounts with those things, so that instantly, right now, and not waiting until we have got over the violent reaction and sting of our mistake and feel a bit better, that precious Blood must be appropriated to deal with that.

Let us remember that all this persistence of the enemy to lay us low has something more in view than just laying us low. It is to destroy our spiritual vocation in prayer and thereby to give him opportunity for assaulting and oppressing the saints. We are responsible for the life and deliverance of the Lord's people. That is what we are here for.

THE CHURCH AND THE POWER OF THE THRONE

Seeing that is so, it is necessary for us always to bear in mind that, while for ourselves, as sinners, God's throne is a throne of grace, it is also a throne of judgment for the enemy. What to us is the throne of grace is the throne of destruction to Satan. We have not only to come in boldness to the throne of grace for ourselves and for the Lord's people needing grace, we have with equal boldness to come to that same throne as the throne which spells the undoing of Satan. Always remember there are two sides to that throne. There is the grace side and the judgment side; the grace side for us because of the precious Blood, and the judgment side for the Adversary.

This latter aspect of the throne is that which comes so prominently into view with Esther. It had to do with the undoing of Haman's devices. We have to recognize that the throne has not only to be in the midst of the Church as the throne of grace, but in all its meaning as the throne of Divine power for undoing the work of Satan. It is a different aspect of prayer, a very important one. You and I should know the touch with the throne against the enemy on behalf of the Lord's people. That throne must be in the Church.

A FINAL WORD ON THE TRUST COMMITTED
TO THE CHURCH

Well now, we must close, and we do so by just gathering it up in this way. This whole trust of the life of the people of God is given to the Church. That is a tremendous thing to say, and an equally tremendous thing to contemplate. I know that, in a very true sense, all is secured in Christ in glory, but it is equally true, according to Divine revelation, that there has to be an outworking, and this latter is committed to the Church. We are workers together with God. We were created in Christ Jesus unto good works which God foreordained that we should walk in them. The Lord has put this tremendous trust upon His people, the working out of His purpose, which is the deliverance and life of His people unto that glorious consummation—the display of the greatness of Christ in His people, through His people.

You see, when Christ comes, He is not just coming to be seen in glory, to be manifested as the glorified, glorious Christ; not just that. He is coming to be glorified *in* His saints and to be marvelled at *in* all them that believe. Christ's glorification is to be something in the Church at last. Unto that, you and I and all the Lord's people are given the trust of working it out. The Lord gives us light. Then, while He is not out of touch with us, in a sense He stands back and says, Now then, that is your business; I have given you light, now get on with it! We are all the time appealing back to the Lord to do it. Lord, come in and do this! Lord, come in and do that! The Lord's attitude is, Get on with it! I am here, I give you the supply of the Spirit, but I have made known to you what your business is: Do your business!

Oh, that the Lord's people would rise up and recognize that He has committed to them this great trust of working out His purpose, of ministering to the life of His people unto that glorious consummation, when the very greatness of Christ shall be displayed in that people. That is our business; and so it is not for us continually to appeal to the Lord for Him to do it as apart from us, but for us to get to the business of prayer and intercession, and in this way minister His life to His people, bring about the deliverance of His people by prayer, standing in touch with His throne for their deliverance from the Evil One and the power of death.

Now, if the very deliverance and life of God's people is at our door by God's appointment, that is no small thing. I believe that the Word clearly reveals that the Church exists for the purpose of taking up this question of the Lord's glory, the Lord's triumph, the Lord's greatness, as that which is to be ultimately displayed in the triumph of His people. It is our responsibility. The Lord give us grace to accept it and to commit ourselves to it, and may we be very much before Him that we shall be found, not as those coerced to pray, but marked by the spirit of intercession as the very evidence of our life.

CHAPTER FOUR

A REPRESENTATION OF CHRIST IN EVERY PLACE

*And Simon Peter answered and said, Thou art the
Christ, the Son of the living God. And Jesus
answered and said unto him, Blessed art thou,
Simon Bar-Jonah: for flesh and blood hath not
revealed it unto thee, but my Father who is in
heaven. And I also say unto thee, that thou art
Peter, and upon this rock I will build my church;
and the gates of Hades shall not prevail against it*
(Matthew 16:16-18, A.S.V.).

*And if he refuse to hear them, tell it unto the
church: and if he refuse to hear the church also,
let him be unto thee as the Gentile and the publican* (Matthew 18:17, A.S.V.).

*For where two or three are gathered together in my
name, there am I in the midst of them*
(Matthew 18:20).

*Now ye are the body of Christ, and members each
in his part* (1 Corinthians 12:27, R.V. Margin).

*...being built upon the foundation of the apostles
and prophets, Christ Jesus himself being the chief
corner stone; in whom each several building, fitly
framed together, groweth into a holy temple in the
Lord; in whom ye also are builded together for a
habitation of God in the Spirit*
(Ephesians 2:20-22, A.S.V.).

As he is, even so are we in this world
(1 John 4:17, A.S.V.).

In continuing our meditation in connection with the spiritual house, I have an emphasis now in my heart which I feel
peculiarly to be of the Lord. For quite a few, it will be no new
word or truth, but even for such the fresh emphasis may be of
the Lord. In any case, they must seek to co-operate in the word
of the Lord for those for whom He may specially mean it. Let
us, nevertheless, all seek to enter into the word in a new way.

We are looking at some of the major features and purposes
of God's spiritual house to which we belong, and the one
which is to occupy us now is this, that this spiritual house is
here as being a representation of Christ in every place. We
have seen that the Church is Christ. He is the Church, He is
God's temple, God's dwelling place. It is in Him that we find
God. He serves the purpose of all that the Church is intended
to mean. The Church is Christ. But now, so far as this world is
concerned, the Church is Christ as distributed, though not
divided; that is, Christ as in all His members by His Spirit; yet
not so many Christs, but remaining one Christ. The Apostle
raised the question amongst the Corinthians, as you know—Is

Christ divided?—and there is almost a tone of scandal at the very idea that Christ should be divided. He remains one, and He is one, though in so many, and in that oneness of Christ in all His members we have the Church. Men will only find the Lord, where we are concerned, so far as Christ is in us. That is the purpose of the Church.

THE VITAL CHARACTER OF THE LOCAL ASSEMBLY

But now we come to consider the special importance of local corporate expressions of Christ, Christ as represented corporately in every place. It is a well-known and understood thing among us that what the Lord Jesus said as recorded in the Gospels was but the truth in germ form. Because the Spirit was not yet given, He could only speak as in an objective way, putting things in a figurative form or in an undeveloped way. All that is in the Gospels is like that, awaiting the day of the Spirit's dwelling within believers so that the much larger meaning contained in His utterances might be imparted. And, amongst all the rest, there is this fragment which we have read in Matthew 18:20—"For where two or three are gathered together in my name, there am I in the midst of them." We shall lose a very great deal if we take that simply as it stands in the Gospel. It was never intended to be taken just in that form.

In the later revelation of the Holy Spirit, that passage, with all others, is taken up and its earlier meaning is made clear, and what we have as the fuller revelation is this, that Christ is peculiarly present when two or three are gathered together, because He has committed Himself to His Body. To put that round the other way, it is the Body of Christ which is necessary for the bringing in of the fulness of Christ. "The body," says the Apostle, "is not one member, but many" (1 Corinthians 12:14). But then the same Apostle says, "Ye are the body of Christ" (1 Corinthians 12:27); and he is speaking of a local company. Christ is peculiarly present when it is a corporate expression. The Lord has bound Himself up with His Church for manifestation. It may be true that the Lord is in us individually; it is true; and it may equally be true that the Lord, as in us individually, will express Himself in us and through us as individuals, but the Lord is limited, and very severely limited, when it is only an individual matter. His thought is otherwise, and so He makes this statement. He might have left a thing like this unsaid. It would seem to have been quite unnecessary, quite beside the mark. But no, He said it, and when He has said a thing, it means something. Indeed, it bears all the significance of such a One as He is having said it. That means it carries tremendous weight if He says it; and He has said this thing in these precise words—"Where two or three are gathered together in my name, there am I in the midst of them." He might have said, Wherever there is one in My Name, there am I! Well, that is true, but the Lord did not put it in that way; and you notice that He is dealing with practical matters. He has used the word "Church." Certain people have to be dealt with by the Church, and when the Church deals with them, it is the Lord. That is what He is saying.

You must bring these two things together. Here is someone guilty of remissness in spiritual life. Well, someone go and tell him, and if he does not hear, take one or two more, and if he refuse to hear them, tell it to the Church.

> *If he refuse to hear the church also, let him be*
> *unto thee as the Gentile and the publican. Verily I*
> *say unto you, what things soever ye shall bind on*

earth shall be bound in heaven; and what things soever ye shall loose on earth shall be loosed in heaven. Again I say unto you, that if two of you shall agree on earth as touching anything that they shall ask, it shall be done for them of my Father who is in heaven. For where two or three are gathered together in my name, there am I in the midst of them (Matthew 18:17-20 A.S.V.).

The Lord is in the midst in an executive way in the Church's administration, where two or three are gathered together. I am not going to deal with that phase of Church functioning, but I use it to bring out this principle, that there is a specific value bound up with a corporate expression of Christ, and a value of very great importance.

Some Fatal Hindrances to God's Purpose

(a) Individualism

Now, let me stop here for a parenthesis. There are some fatal mistakes into which Christians have fallen, and one of these is the principle of the individual line in the place of the corporate. I say that has been a fatal mistake. It has been fatal to spiritual growth, fatal to spiritual fulness, to spiritual power, to spiritual light and to spiritual life. There are many Christians who are only concerned with individuals. Concern for the individual is of course right, but the Lord only saves the individual with the Church in view, with the corporate Body in mind. We must settle it and be very clear that this dispensation, from the ascension and exaltation of Christ, and the giving of the Holy Spirit, to the taking away of the Church at the end, is marked out by God as the period in all the periods of this world's history for securing, not individuals as so many saved men and women, but as one Body—the Church. Individuals only figure before God in the light of the Church, the one Body, and, if you and I fail to recognize that as the governing law of God's dealings with men in this dispensation, we are going to forfeit a great measure of what the Lord intended for us; limit and straiten our spiritual lives and experiences, and cause weakness in the very work of God itself.

I hope you have understood that. It is of very great importance that we should settle this. You will notice that these two things usually go together. It is the salvation of the individual that engages and occupies so many, and when they have got the individual saved, brought to the Lord, they have no further concern but to go and get more individuals and bring them into salvation. Those two things go together, individualism and salvation in its merely initial sense of souls being brought to the Lord. After that, there is no more. That has proved a fatal thing in the history of God's interests, and to-day we are finding it to be one of the things which is representing the greatest difficulty to Christians themselves and to any fuller work of God. I mean this, that you everywhere meet a large number of people who have just gone that far. All that they have is just their own personal salvation, in the sense of forgiveness of sins, peace with God, those rudiments of the Gospel, and they have been there ten, twenty, thirty, forty, fifty years; and to-day as you meet them and speak with them, you come up against one of two things.

On the one hand, there is an utter inability now to apprehend anything more than the simple elements of salvation; they have not got ability to do it. All those spiritual senses and faculties which ought to have been developed so that they could receive much larger and fuller revelation from God have been stunted, have never been developed by exercise, and in spiritual faculties they remain simply infants after all these years. I am only giving you the Scripture in saying that. You know, Paul had to say that very thing to the Corinthians—"I... could not speak unto you as unto spiritual, but as unto carnal, as unto babes in Christ. I fed you with milk, not with meat" (1 Corinthians 3:1 A.S.V.). To the Hebrews it was the same: "When by reason of the time ye ought to be teachers, ye have need again that some one teach you the rudiments of the first principles of the oracles of God; and are become such as have need of milk....solid food is for fullgrown men, even those who by reason of use have their senses exercised to discern good and evil."

Paul had to deplore in his own day that there had been this fatal arrest and he said, in effect, Here I am, just full of Divine light for you, and I have to keep back all this that God has given me for His Church because of that! I say that is fatal for the Church—that the Lord should give abundant revelation for His Church's growth and fulness and functioning, and that there should be, after years and years and years, such a state that people are totally incapable in themselves of receiving it, understanding it. You meet that condition to-day everywhere. They cannot, after so long a time.

On the other hand, of course, you find those who after a lifetime turn to you and say, Oh, that I had known this before! Oh, that I had been told this before! Oh, that I had had this years ago! Why not? It has been here all the time. It is because of this fatal individualistic line. For the greater part, the work of God since the early days of the Church, with the exception of very small things here and there, has been just on this line of getting individuals saved and leaving them there. It is fatal in the long run to all that God intended; and then people come up against the fact that it is so. Oh, that I had known it long ago! Well then, while the individual is very important, and has to be dealt with in the light of the other as an individual, we must note that, if the individual is put in the place of the corporate, nothing but the most sorrowful consequences can follow. That is one fatal mistake.

(B) THE PREVAILING "CHURCH SYSTEM"

Another fatal thing is that which is represented by the present "Church system." The present system which obtains in the largest realm is almost entirely a matter of congregations and preaching places, places where people gather together or congregate in a religious way—yes, maybe an evangelical way, yet but congregations—and they come together to go through a certain rota and, in the main, to hear something preached, and they go away. Now, while there are variations and degrees in that system, that very largely is the position; and that is not a corporate expression of Christ. That is a congregation. That is not a body. That is not the Body locally expressed and functioning. It is something less. What is the result? The same result as in the other case, namely, very little spiritual growth.

I am being very frank now. I want to talk out of my heart because I feel the Lord wants to get us somewhere in this hour on this matter, and I must run the risk of treading upon sensibilities in order to get there. The result spiritually in this second instance is very largely the same as in the other case of the merely individualistic, and we are everywhere finding people to-day in that present Church system who have not a glimmer of light on the Lord's fuller purpose and do not know what you are talking about; and multitudes of them have no interest in anything else. This thing, this going to church, this congregation, this going through a rota, this place of the public worship line of things has come into the place of the true local expression of the Body of Christ, and has set that aside. To-day, speaking of the Church in that sense, it is the Church like that which is in a state of terrible spiritual infancy and immaturity and unenlightenment after all these centuries, and people born and brought up in it do not grow spiritually. I know there are some who do grow despite it, but I am speaking of the thing itself. It has become a fatal menace to the real purpose of God.

(c) The Making of "The Gospel Mission" to Be Everything

Now, there is a third thing, and that is "The Gospel Mission," which also takes the place of the local church as spiritually formed. Now, this is no denunciation of Gospel Missions, and I am not saying that Gospel Missions ought not to be. I am far, very far from saying that. I am, of course, not speaking now of those evangelistic missions that are held among the churches from time to time, but of that which has assumed the character of a permanent institution in numerous places. If then you take the Gospel Mission and have that as though it were everything that there is, and you remain satisfied just to go to the Gospel Mission where the Gospel is preached to the unsaved, and keep on the Gospel Mission line of things; well, you are simply dwarfing your own spiritual life. It is a thing which has in multitudes of cases just become a substitute for the spiritually formed local expression of Christ.

Christ is much more than that, and you note that the people who live all their lives in the Gospel Mission are the people who are most terribly immature, spiritually ignorant and unenlightened. Oh yes, rejoicing in Christ as their Saviour—I do not question that—glorying in personal salvation; but oh, where is vocation, where is the fulness of Christ, where is God's eternal purpose being worked out? Not there. That just goes one step, and one step is not the whole road to God's end. Let there be these things, but let them be as auxiliaries to the fuller thought of God, as instrumentalities of the Church, and let them not be the whole thing. If they are, they will fatally affect the life of God's people and spiritual progress.

You see, the difference is this. Take a bunch of flowers, a bunch of roses or any other particular kind of flower. They are of the same species, and they have the same life in them. That is a congregation, not a body! The difference between a bunch of flowers which are all alike, all sharing the same life, and the root and the plant, is a very big one. Give me the rose, root and plant or bush, and what shall I have? Well, I shall have this difference that, whereas the bunch of flowers has the life, it just goes so far. That is all and there it ends. It will never go beyond that. Give me the plant or bush, and it will grow. It may pass through a paroxysm of death for a season, but next year it will come back again and there will be more; and then another experience of dying and resurrection, and again there will be more, all in the same plant. That is a body, that is an organism, not a bunch. And that is the difference between a congregation, so many Christians, units coming together as units, and a spiritual organism, a local expression of the Body of Christ; and it is the Body which is God's thought, not a congregation, not the bunch of flowers.

But oh, the Lord's people are so much like the bunch of flowers! It is true they are all of the same species: They are Christians, they are children of God, they are all sharing the same life; but oh, they are not there as one organism in one place growing with the increase of God, passing through corporate convulsions of death and resurrection and making spiritual increase in that way. What I have said about the present system and the missions is just like a bunch of flowers. Yes, they belong to the Lord, and they have the same life, they are all the Lord's children; but they just come to a certain point and they never go beyond that. That is true. I have had enough experience to make me sure it is true. Alas, many of them do not want to go any further, and many of them resent the suggestion that it is necessary to go any further. However, that is not God's thought about it. God's thought is of the root and the plant as a whole, a living organism here and there as representing and expressing Christ Himself. The plant grows and makes increase. The bunch simply goes so far and then it stops.

Now, Satan is not adverse to meetings as such, but Satan is adverse to local families, local expressions of the Body of Christ. Hence you have the great history of Satan's persistent effort to scatter the children of God and break up their corporate life, to bring an end to their practical functioning together.

THE PURPOSE AND FUNCTION OF THE CHURCH, AS ALSO OF ITS LOCAL EXPRESSION

So we have to see exactly what the purpose and the function of a local expression of the Body or the Church or House of God really is, and we can see it if we look at the type that leads to the antitype. What the temple of old was in figure, the Church is in spiritual reality, and what the Church is in spiritual reality as a whole, the local company is to be. It is remarkable that local churches in the New Testament are always viewed in the light of the whole Body. Thus Paul will say to the local church at Corinth, "Ye are the body of Christ." Now, it would not do for Corinth to take hold of that and say, You see, *we* are the Body of Christ! That would be giving a wrong meaning to it. The point in the inspired declaration is this, that every local company is in representation what the whole Body is; what the whole Body is in God's thought is to be seen here and there and there.

(A) The Meeting Place Between God and Man

Now we continue by way of analogy from the temple. What was the temple? In the first place, the temple of old was the meeting place between God and man. That is the first function of the temple, of the House of God. Christ was that in the fullest sense, in a far greater sense than was ever temple of old. Here is Son of Man and Son of God blended in one Person. It is tremendously significant that in Matthew 16. that very fact comes to light. Christ, interrogating His disciples, uses one term, and, in getting the Divinely-inspired response through Peter, the other term is used. "Who do men say that the Son of man is?" Peter said, "Thou art the Son of the living God." "Son of man," "Son of God": and that is by revelation of God. Here is God and Man met together in one Person, in one place. And of Himself the Lord Jesus later said, Destroy this temple, this sanctuary, and in three days I will raise it up again. Carnally minded Jews thought He was speaking of that material temple, but He was speaking of Himself, His own body. This temple—transition of thought from the temple in

Jerusalem to Christ personally, the meeting place of God and man—that is Christ.

Now Christ corporately expressed is the Church according to revelation in the New Testament, and therefore where Christ is corporately found in representation, and livingly functioning, there God should be met with, there God and man should come into a peculiar touch and relationship. The testimony of all who come into such a realm where Christ is really corporately expressed ought to be, I find the Lord there! and that ought to be enough. That is the answer. Do you find the Lord there? Does the Lord meet with you there? Ah, that is the first governing thing, and not other questions associated with gathering together or congregations; no, the Lord Himself, and that not now as a personal thing between myself and the Lord, seeing that I personally can have touch with the Lord anywhere, but now as a matter of the Church. Do I meet the Lord in the midst of that people? If so, I have come into the realm where God's thought is having expression; and that is a realm of tremendous possibilities.

> The testimony of all who come into such a realm where Christ is really corporately expressed ought to be, I find the Lord there!

Have you read that little book by A.J. Gordon, *How Christ Came to Church*? It might do you good to read it, though rather perhaps from an objective or outside point of view. But let me tell you as quickly as I can the content. Dr. Gordon one Saturday was sitting preparing his sermon for the following day in his study, when he fell asleep; and he dreamt that he was in his own church and in his pulpit on the Lord's day. His was a very fine church with its Gothic pillars and arches. The church was crowded, and he was in the pulpit about to commence the service, when the door opened at the back and a stranger entered and walked down the aisle looking from side to side for a seat. As he got nearer the front, someone stepped out and showed him a vacant seat.

Dr. Gordon goes on to describe how he went on with the service, and how his eyes constantly turned to that stranger. If he looked in some other way, he found his eyes coming back to him. Dr. Gordon said, "I registered the resolve that I would go down to speak to the stranger after the service." After it was over, and without showing noticeable hurry, he just as quickly as he could made his way down and tried to intercept the stranger, but before he reached the door, the stranger was gone. With great disappointment, he said to the man at the door, Do you know who that stranger was you let in this morning? The man at the door said, Don't you know who that was? That was Jesus of Nazareth. Oh, said Dr. Gordon, why did you not detain Him? I would love to have spoken to Him. Oh, said the man, do not worry; He was here to-day, He will come again. (Well, as an aside, that double reply bore fruit in two volumes from Dr. Gordon's pen; the one on *The Work of the Holy Spirit*, and the other on *The Coming of the Lord*.)

Dr. Gordon says he went away with these musings—Jesus of Nazareth has been in my church to-day. What was I saying? I was talking about Him. How did I talk about Him? Did He discern in anything that I was saying the faintest tinge of unreality? Did I speak of Him, not knowing He was present, as I would have if I had known? What did He think of my manner, my matter, my conducting of the service? What did He think about our choir, our singing? It was all about Him, but was it worthy of Him? I wonder what He thought about our Gothic building?

That is the story in brief. But what has come to me is this: Is that our conception of things? You see, in that the suggestion is that the Church is one thing and Christ another, and that the Church can be in all sorts of respects certain things, and Christ quite another. Oh no, that is not God's Church. God's Church is Christ, and where you find the Church according to God, there you find Christ, and no disparities, no inconsistencies, contradictions; it is the Lord. All the other is not Christ at all. The Church is Christ, and if it is Christ who is preeminent when the Lord's people come together, God is there Himself. It is on the ground of Christ and Christ's presence that men meet with God. You know as well as I do that men cannot meet with God in us as we are. We cannot of ourselves bring men into touch with God. No priesthood as such can bring men to God. But if the Lord Jesus is in us, and we can bring men into touch with the Lord Jesus, we have brought them into touch with God. But if He is not there in us either personally or collectively, we may talk about God till Doomsday, but men will not meet Him. That is what the Church is when truly constituted. It is the ground upon which men meet God and God meets men, and that ground is Christ Himself; and there is peculiar and special value and significance bound up with this corporate expression of Christ in the matter of men meeting God. I believe that a far greater impact of the Lord can be registered upon men by a company of Christ-indwelt men and women being together in the power of the Holy Spirit than can be by any number of isolated Christian units. A meeting place between God and man, the vehicle of Divine life.

You see Ezekiel's temple. The house is now finished according to God's mind, and it is out from the house, down the steps, the river flows, deepening and widening on its way, and wheresoever the river cometh everything lives. Trees are seen on either bank and everything is living, until at length it empties itself into the Dead Sea; and even that death is swallowed up in the life that is out from the sanctuary. It is this corporate expression of Christ, the Church, from which there is the ministration of God's life to men, and that is why the enemy wants to break it up. That was our point in our previous meditation. The scattering or dividing of the Lord's people, the making of the Lord's people into so many individuals and units alone, without a real corporate life, is a strategical move on the part of the enemy against that life. We know in our own experience that, if the enemy can get in between even two of us to set us apart in spirit, our life is under arrest and the river is not released until we mend that bridge, heal that division. That is very significant. The enemy is after that sort of thing. He is against the life, because the Church is the vehicle of God's life.

(B) The Embodiment and Expression of God's Thoughts

Then again, the temple was the embodiment and expression of God's thoughts. Every stone, everything used, all sizes, dimensions and measurements, materials, they all represented some thought of God. God's mind was expressed in all. It was a symbol of a spiritual attribute.

Peter, following up that word which is before us—"a spiritual house" (1 Peter 2:5, A.S.V.) says a little later that the object of the spiritual house is to "show forth the excellencies of him who called you out of darkness into his marvellous light." The temple was to show forth the excellencies of the Lord, the embodiment of Divine thoughts, and the Lord's people in any place should be the embodiment and expression of Divine thoughts. There should be there a disclosing of God's thoughts in a very blessed way, a coming to know the mind of the Lord for His people, a rich unveiling of what is in the heart of God concerning His own. That is how it ought to be; not just addresses or sermons, but a ministry of revelation under the Holy Spirit through an opened heaven. That is of value to the Lord and to His people. But it wants a living company for that; and oh, how we know it! Sometimes we are not all alive to the Lord for some reason or other when we come together. Perhaps we are tired, or have been bothered, something has come in to cast down, and although the Lord has prepared for us some rich feast, something He wants to make known, He cannot; He is held back, and there is just a state of lifelessness. But let us come together in the Spirit, alive unto the Lord, and the Lord's thoughts come out and they flow. The condition of the company of the Lord's people very largely determines what kind of time we have. It very largely depends upon us how much the Lord can give us. The company of the Lord's people is to be the expression and embodiment of God's thoughts. That is what it exists for.

(C) THE SPHERE OF DIVINE GOVERNMENT AND AUTHORITY

Then the temple was the place of God's government. Things were brought there to be decided upon, to be judged: and Peter says, "Judgment must begin at the house of God"; and that is Matthew 18 again. Tell it to the Church, let the Church decide on this. It is the place of Divine government. I cannot stay with that, but you see that the corporate company, living-ly constituted according to Christ, is of very real and practical

consequence to God in this world now: and oh, how important it is for life's sake, for light's sake, for power's sake, that
we all be consciously and livingly a part of such a local expression of God.

I do want to say this to you from my heart, that it is necessary for you, dear friends, to be a part of, to be in the midst
of, to have behind you, a living, functioning company of the
Lord's people on this basis. I know the difference, and many
of you know the difference, the difference it makes in depth,
in strength. For many years, I was a minister, as we say, of different churches, congregations; but oh, I know the difference
between that and what has obtained since. It is not a difference of the natural calibre of the people at all, but a difference
in kind. The one was a part of a system largely organized and
run by man for religious purposes: the other is something
formed of the Spirit; and that is an immense difference. I know
the difference when I meet things. All you can say is that those
who have a living local company of the Lord's people of
whom they are a part, have something that other people have
not. There is measure about them. There is something about
them that is more than you will find in the other things of
which I have spoken, where it is purely individualistic or formal. It is very important. The Church is intended to be this,
and a thing can only know its Divinely appointed resources as
it functions according to God's intention. If therefore we are
called for this as the Church, then we must be the Church in
order to fulfil our great purpose and know our great fulness. I
do ask you to think about this very seriously. It is a thing of
no little importance, is this matter of the local fellowship of the
Lord's people.

I know it may raise problems for some of you. "There is nothing in our neighbourhood and I do not know how it is possible." But there is an answer, and the answer is a simple one, although it may test you. If this is God's mind, you go to the Lord about it. "Lord, if this is Your mind, either bring me into such a thing or bring about such a thing where I am." Hold on to the Lord for that.

Brother Nee, when he was here, speaking about this matter and talking with one and another about it, spoke of how in one place this very thing arose between someone and the Lord, and how that one held on to the Lord for several years over the matter; and then how that, after holding on for so long, gradually the formation commenced, a second being joined to the first, and then a third, and then another. But they were greatly exercised for a long time, standing themselves into the meaning and value of God's thought and holding on to Him for it to find expression and become a reality. You see, that is just it. That is our ministry; through prayer to bring into being what God intends. If we can be put off easily, well then, we have not seen the vision, the thing has not gone very deep. That is only said by way of helping with the problem that arises. Let us be exercised about the Church and let the Church be of greater importance to us than the problem, then I think we shall find a way through.

CHAPTER FIVE

THE GOVERNING LAW OF THE HOUSE OF GOD

Reading: Ezekiel 47:1-12; 1 Peter 2:4-5.

We are not going forward now with a further consideration of the major features of the spiritual house of God, but are leaving that for another time. We are going to bring those features already considered to the measuring line of their own governing law, which is that of life and spirituality. "Living," "spiritual," they are two great words in this passage—"a living stone," "living stones," "a spiritual house," "spiritual sacrifices."

Lest anyone should be in difficulty about that second word, "spirituality," let us stay for the briefest moment to say that spirituality just means government by the Holy Spirit; but a government by the Holy Spirit in such a way as to make us one with the Holy Spirit in all His standards, in all His ways of looking at things, deciding about things, so that, being one with Him, we are not at all influenced or affected by natural judgments, natural standards, natural considerations, but ours are all the Holy Spirit's judgments and values and ways of viewing things. That in brief and comprehensively is what is meant by spirituality, a constituting of us according to the Holy Spirit, which means on the other hand, the ruling out of all that is merely and purely of our own natural life, mind, heart and will.

Well now, let us look at these four features of the spiritual house of God, which house we are if we are the Lord's, and look at them in the light of life and spirituality.

THE EXALTATION OF THE LORD JESUS

The first with which we were concerned was that this spiritual house of God exists for the purpose of setting forth, proclaiming, manifesting the exaltation of the Lord Jesus as God's Son, the exaltation of the Lord Jesus to the throne of the Father. It is for that the Church exists, and it is for that we exist if we are of the house of God. But that is not just a truth, a doctrine to be proclaimed. That is not just a part of the Church's creed—"Jesus Christ has been raised from the dead and exalted to the right hand of the Majesty on high." That is not just one of our convictions, as we say. That is something which has to constitute us spiritually and has to be expressed by means of life. The exaltation of the Lord Jesus is, before and above all other things, a matter of life. It was when He was exalted to the right hand of the Majesty on high, it was when God made Him both Lord and Christ, it was when He was actually seated at God's right hand, far above all rule and authority, principalities and powers, that the Holy Spirit came out from His presence and made that which was in Heaven, a spiritual reality in the Church; and that reality was marked and demonstrated and proved and evidenced by the mighty power of His ascended life. We have to be spiritually constituted on

the basis of Christ's exaltation. That is to say, within us something has to be done that brings about in us a living spiritual
oneness with the exaltation, the Lordship, the supremacy of
Jesus Christ. It is not to remain something outside of us, however true it is.

We have to be that in fact; and, as we have pointed out, the
impact of the early believers upon this world, upon those
around them wherever they were, was the impact of the *fact*,
not the doctrine, not the teaching, not merely the statement,
but the *fact* that Jesus Christ was exalted. That came home
upon the situation because that fact has its supreme significance in the spiritual realm, and we know quite well that all
that is visible, all that is here on this sentient creation, has
behind it a spiritual order.

Never has that been more clearly manifested and demonstrated than in the present world situation. There is a spiritual
order of things which is driving on, mastering, manipulating
everything. It is, as many have been saying for the past
months, Satanic in its background. The exaltation of the Lord
Jesus finds its first registration there, and it is not until the registration is made there that the foreground is really affected. To
arrest men, to arrest a course of things, to bring the yoke down
upon situations, to harness developments in the seen, you
have to get behind and register some superior reality against
those forces that are creating these things.

Now, that is spirituality. The Apostle Paul said much about
this sort of thing, and we have his language by which he
expressed this reality. For example, "the weapons of our warfare are not of the flesh, but mighty before God to the casting
down of strongholds" (2 Corinthians 10:4, A.S.V.). He did not
actually use the word, but it is quite clear that he meant that

the weapons of our warfare are spiritual, getting behind the situation: and you know what he was dealing with at the moment when he used those words. Here were Corinthians who were seeking the advantages of natural wisdom, natural learning, the wisdom and the power of this world, in order to give them position, influence, standing. They were carnal in their quest for carnal weapons by which to gain ascendency in this world. That led the Apostle to that great discourse on the foolishness and the weakness of this world's wisdom and this world's strength, and he said that, to overcome this world, you want something more than this world's weapons, this world's men. To overcome the carnal, you must have something more than carnal weapons, and the weapons of our warfare are not carnal, but mighty through God. In other words, they are spiritual. For our wrestling is not against flesh and blood in the form of wisdom and worldly power, "but against the principalities, against the powers, against the world-rulers of this darkness, against the spiritual hosts of wickedness in the heavenly places" (Ephesians 6:12, A.S.V.).

Therefore our weapons must be spiritual, and spirituality means fundamentally the ability to get behind the seen, the tangible, to the unseen, the invisible, the intangible powers of evil, and to register your superiority there: and that superiority is the exaltation of the Lord Jesus far above all rule and authority and principality and power. That is a spiritual thing.

The house of God is a spiritual house for that spiritual purpose, namely, to bring home Christ's ascendency in a spiritual way against spiritual forces. Then the instrumentalities of those evil spiritual forces will in turn come under arrest. It is no use going directly at things. You must strike at the cause of things, and then the things themselves will, according to God's purpose and intention, either be destroyed, or be brought under arrest or limitation, just as the Lord intends. It is not the Lord's thought to stop wars altogether just yet, nor much else that is going on in an evil way, but there is such a thing as limiting things to the purpose of God; and I do feel, and appeal to you as the Lord's children, that we ought to be engaged in this spiritual registration of the authority and supremacy of the Lord Jesus in the unseen, in the background of present world situations, with the object of limiting things to God's purpose.

I believe it is possible for the Lord's people now to take hold of every air raid on this country and limit it, give it God's limitation, and I believe that that is what is happening. I only use it by way of illustrating my point. It is an amazing thing how things have been limited. We have seen again and again what might have been, and how much the onslaught has been penned in, even where great damage has been done. Oh, how much more might have been, could have been, and the amazement of every day is the limitation that is imposed. Surely that is an encouragement. I believe it is due to something in the unseen that is set in motion through the prayers of the people of God. That is encouraging. Let us be given to our ministry. That is what the Church is for.

Thus the very first thing is that Jesus is exalted above all principality and powers which lie behind this world darkness, and the Church is here, by prayer and testimony and spiritual life, to bring home upon those background forces this superiority of the Lord Jesus. It is a thing, not of words, not of doctrines, not of creeds, but of life, the impact of His ascended life.

Well, we begin there. The principle, you see, the law of the expression of Christ's exaltation, is life and spirituality.

THE MINISTRY OF THE HOUSE OF GOD

The second thing which we were noticing with regard to these features of the spiritual house of God was that it exists to minister to the pleasure and glory of God. It is for God's glory, God's pleasure that the Church has been brought into being, for His satisfaction. And here we bring it right down to this rule: God is glorified and God receives that which is to His pleasure along the line of life and spirituality. You can judge of that by the effect. Wherever you have a real ministration of life, you always have the glory of God, God glorified.

That is, of course, true to the Scriptures. You remember that was the one point which the Lord Jesus made central and supreme in the raising of Lazarus. "This sickness is not unto death, but for the glory of God"; and as He came through all the doubt and unbelief which stood between Him and Lazarus, and approached the situation, at least He silently lifted His heart to the Father. "Father, glorify thy name!" Then He cried with a loud voice, "Lazarus, come forth!" The resurrection of Lazarus, the overpowering of death, was for the glory of God, and that was a spiritual thing, that was the triumph of life in Christ. Now, that is the glory of God. It says afterward that many believed on Him. The glory of God is largely seen through the outworking of this principle of life triumphant over death.

Now, that is a big subject. If you go back to the Old Testament, you will see that, in the case of every servant of God, after that servant of God was apprehended by Him, a process of death and resurrection commenced. You can take any one case that you like. Outstandingly, there is Abraham. How significant are the words that mark the apprehending of that servant of God. "The God of glory appeared unto our father Abraham" (Acts 7:2). That sets the standard of God, and in effect says, Now then, it is according to what I am as the God of glory that I am going to deal with you, and the issue of all My dealings with you will be glory to Me! So, no sooner was Abraham apprehended by the God of glory, than this process of death and resurrection set in. It was a process with constant recurrence. Abraham went into a first stage and phase and measure of death, and then, in resurrection, the glory of God was seen. All the way along, there was this experience of death.

I am not speaking now about physical death, but of a working of death in his life in a spiritual way; death to things, death to relationships, death to hopes, death to earthly expectations, death to possessions; and every time death worked, there was a resurrection into something larger of the Lord, the Lord coming and making new covenants, giving him fresh revelations. I am El Shaddai! There were all these positive things when other things were going into death, right up to that last great triumph of resurrection in Isaac. Here is death; yes, death to all the promises, apparently, to all the hopes. If Isaac goes, then God in His faithfulness, God in His Word, God in His covenant, God in His promises, has gone too. It was a mighty death to face, and in spirit it was faced, but it was resurrection finally, full, glorious resurrection: and what glory to God!

Well, you can take many other illustrations of the truth from the Old Testament and then carry them over in a spiritual way to the New Testament, and see that this is exactly what happened with Christ. God received the full quota of glory through the death and the resurrection of His Son, and the exaltation of the Lord Jesus is the testimony to the fact that death has been engulfed and overpowered. Christ being there sets forth that fact in fulness. But then the principle has to be passed on to the Church which is His Body, and the history of the Church since that time has been just a history of successive deaths and resurrections, and every resurrection has meant some fresh contribution to the glory of God, some fresh expression of God's glory; and what is true of the history of the Church is true in the history of many an individual member of the Church, and probably of some of you. We have known deaths oft, not in the way in which Paul meant, physical and temporal and natural, but in our own life with God we have known what it means to suffer the eclipse of all things, darkness unto death. But that has not been the end. The end has been the God of glory again and again, and it is along this line that God's glory is ministered to, by life, spirituality, and life triumphing over death. We are here for that very purpose. I hope that does not discourage you, but rather that it will help you to recognize that our very being here means that we have to know death again and again to know life. But we do not end with death; we end with resurrection and glory to God. Let us fasten upon that. Even though the deaths may be many, the end is the glory of God. Eventually, His glory will be displayed in His Son, in His Church, in fulness, when death is finally vanquished, not only in Christ, but in and through the Church.

But this is something for present experience. It is a great truth to contemplate, it is a blessed thing to consider; but let us bring it right home. What I feel to be the important thing now, the Lord's desire where this hour is concerned, is that we should come very close to these things in reality; that what we are saying shall not be truth only, but reality in our case. We are the house of God, we are this spiritual house, and we exist for this very purpose, to minister to the pleasure and glory of God, and that is done along the line of life, and that life is the life which overcomes death. So that, with every fresh uprising and experience of spiritual death, we shall write over it, This is not unto death, but for the glory of God! Oh, may He give us grace to do that. It is easier said than done, I know, but here it is. History sets the seal to this, that this is the way in which the Lord is ministered to in satisfaction and glory, by our being the very vessel in which the power of His resurrection is manifested, and that necessitates experiences of death.

THE MINISTRY OF THE HOUSE TO THE ELECT

Then the third feature of this spiritual house is that it stands for the deliverance and life of others, the others being, of course, God's elect, those who are bound up with God's eternal purpose. We are here to serve the Lord in standing over against the persistent and determined purpose of Satan to bring an end to Christ's life in His Church, and the test of the reality, the spiritual reality, of this spiritual house is just in this direction, how much are we ministering to the life of God's people to deliver them from these recurrent onslaughts of spiritual death? That is the test. We have to get right up close to that. It is all very well to talk about these things, but they have to be true really. It should become impossible to deal with these matters merely as the teaching that goes on in a certain place. The teaching may be all right, quite correct, but what of the practical issue, so far as we are concerned as the Lord's people? The test is not whether we have accepted right doctrine: the test is whether we are functioning according to what we are, whether we are really doing the thing which constitutes our very existence.

You see, the Church, the people of God, are not one thing, and the truth another thing, and the Church accepts that truth.

It is not that. It is that the Church is that truth or it is nothing at all. I say I am a member of Christ's Body. Well then, I can take the attitude that certain truths are the truths which belong to members of Christ's Body, and therefore I accept those truths: I assent to those truths and henceforth I believe in those truths, and I begin to preach them. That is one thing. Another way is that certain truths are realities concerning the members of Christ's Body, and you cannot divide between the truths and the members, and the very existence of those members means that those truths are operating, and if those truths are not operating, you have serious reason to question the reality of the life of that member of the Body of Christ. Something has gone wrong; it is not normal, it is all wrong. I am not saying that if these truths are not fully manifested in us that has nullified our relationship to Christ as members of His Body, but I am saying that if it is the case that these truths are not being expressed, there is something seriously wrong with us as members of the Body and we are a contradiction to the true meaning of our existence. You and I exist for the life of others and if others are not receiving life through us, then there is something inconsistent in our very existence. That sounds very hard, very severe, but that has to come home to me as much as to you. I never talk to you without having myself very much in mind, and I have this understanding with the Lord, that He will make good all truth in my own case or save me from talking about it.

I challenge you, my dear friends, to face this law of your existence. Are you ministering to the Lord's people or are you merely sitting back, or even worse, ministering death? What does your presence mean to the Lord's people? Does it mean life? If so, then the house of God is truly represented by us. If it does not, if it is only neutral or negative or antagonistic to life, then the house of God has broken down where such are concerned. All these things are a matter of life and spirituality, and there is a horrible thing from which we shall pray earnestly and fervently to be delivered, and that is, talking truth, holding truths, accepting truths, being associated with truths as truths, without having the life of those truths manifested in us. I often fear that is one of the great and distressing things where such revelation exists, that people begin to take up the truths, and they stand for the truths that "Honor Oak" [Honor Oak Baptist Church in London, where Rev. Sparks was a ministered.] stands for. God deliver us from that way of speech and that mentality. That is not it. Either we are this thing, or, however much we may agree with it and talk about it, we are not it.

It is life and spirituality that matters, and we must be much before God that all shall be real in our case; that our presence means that life is ministered, life is passed on. We are the vehicle of life to the Lord's people for their deliverance from the onslaught of death. It was for that Paul besought the believers to pray for him. Oh, this throttling work of the enemy in the matter of ministering life to the Lord's people.

AN EXPRESSION OF CHRIST

Then the fourth thing is that the Church in its corporate life exists to be a present expression of the Lord Jesus Himself wherever two or three are gathered together. I wonder if we have recognized what that word in Matthew 18 really does mean? Here is someone who belongs to the Lord, who is guilty of, or responsible for something wrong. "If thy brother sin against thee." The margin says that a good many authorities omit "against thee." Thus it would read, "If thy brother sin, go, show him his fault...if he hear thee, thou hast gained thy brother. But if he hear thee not, take with thee one or two more, that at the mouth of two witnesses or three every word may be established. And if he refuse to hear them, tell it unto the church: and if he refuse to hear the church also, let him be unto thee as the Gentile and the publican. Verily I say unto you, what things soever ye shall bind on earth shall be bound in heaven; and what things soever ye shall loose on earth shall be loosed in heaven....*For* where two or three are gathered together in my name, there am I in the midst of them" (A.S.V.).

That little word *for* carries with it a tremendous weight of significance. If thy brother sin and after three successive and varied efforts have been made to get him to acknowledge his sin, there is still a withholding, bring it to the Church. Now then, if he refuse to hear the Church, put him out; let him be as a Gentile and a publican, that is, outside the Church; and in your doing that, it is the Lord doing it. "For where two or three are gathered together in my name, there am I in the midst of them." It is not that the Church has acted as something in itself. The Lord regards that as Himself acting. He is there in the midst, and it is the Lord doing this. The Church's verdict is the Lord's verdict; the Church's decision is the Lord's decision, when the Church is gathered into His Name.

Now we can leave the specific connection of that and take up the principle. The Church exists to be a corporate expression of Christ wherever He is represented. The Church cannot be represented with less than two, because the Church is a Body, and one brick never made a temple yet. It is a corporate thing, and it is to be an expression of Christ there in its corporate life. That is the purpose of the Church, to be an expression of Christ. That cannot be just official, that cannot be formal. It is not that the Church has a session and in its session has an agenda and discusses certain propositions and comes to certain decisions. No, it is something much deeper than that.

In the first place, the Church is spiritual, that is, the Church has subjected itself to the Holy Spirit and has taken the Holy Spirit for its governance, for its direction. It has put its trust in the Spirit of God to register right courses and right decisions through much prayer. It has altogether submitted itself to the government of the Holy Spirit and in that way become spiritual, so that it livingly functions in a spiritual way; not formally functions, but spiritually and livingly functions, that is, its function is on the witness of the Spirit along the line of life. Issues are raised, difficulties are brought up. How are these going to be met? Well, someone makes a proposition and those who are spiritual feel, Oh, this is death if we take that line! No, we have no liberty to take that line, that would be terrible! It is registered inside. It is not that we have better judgment, but within the Spirit of life says, Do not take that line, that will be disaster! Or someone else may say something and those who are spiritual feel, Yes, that is the Lord's way! It is registered within; the Spirit of life is governing; and that is the basis of the Church's life altogether, and it becomes in that way an expression of Christ, an expression of the mind of the Lord there. The Lord is in evidence along the line, and on the basis, of life and spirituality. But it requires a corporate life for that—"In the mouth of two or three witnesses." That is the corporate principle, you see, at work. I had no intention of going into so much technique about the Church, but it is all to indicate this great truth, that the Church, this spiritual house, exists to be an expression of Christ wherever it is represented by two or three on a corporate basis.

You see, corporate life is spiritual and is life. It is a matter of life. Our union, our relationship with Christ, is on the principle of life. "Unto whom coming, a living stone...ye also, as living stones, are built up a spiritual house" (A.S.V.). Again I say, God is not dealing with us as bricks; God is dealing with us as with living stones. That means that He is treating us as those who have a common life with the Lord Jesus, and our relationship with the living stone is the relationship of one life. It is a spiritual relationship and it is that life which brings about the corporate expression. It is all the difference between this corporate expression on the basis of life, and a society, a club, an institution. You can join a club, you can come into a society, and you may agree on many things with regard to conviction and procedure, and yet not be bound together by a corporate life. But the Church is this latter thing. One life in all the members links all the members with the Head, and thus by that life it expresses Christ wherever it is. It does not just proclaim things about Christ. It brings Christ in and says that here, though it be but in two or three or more, here Christ has come in. It is not a claim made.

> One life in all the members links all the members with the Head, and thus by that life it expresses Christ wherever it is.

You see, the Roman church will make that claim, that very claim, that where that church is, Christ is. Ah yes, but there is a difference. It is not just a claim, but a fact borne out, that where these spiritual and living stones are, the Lord is there in very truth and people know it, and there comes about that of which the Apostle wrote. When someone comes in from the outside and things are as they should be, when they are after this kind, the outsider comes in and falls down and says, "God is indeed among you." Ah! that is what we want. Whether people begin to fall literally or not, that is not the question. The point is that inwardly they go down; prejudices, suspicions, fears, reservations go down. One thing rises supreme with them and brings down everything. I cannot get away from it, the Lord is there! If only we would surrender to that and all that means it would be very much better for us. But that is the great matter, namely, bringing in the Lord. The Church exists to bring the Lord into every place, even where represented by but two or three. May this all be true in our case. I am sure our hearts respond to that. Well, let us get to the Lord about it, that so far as we individually are concerned as living stones, it may be true in our case; that we are a ministration of life, a representation of Christ, that we are bringing glory to God, that we are setting forth the exaltation of His Son.

CHAPTER SIX

THE SCHOOL OF SONSHIP UNTO ADOPTION

Reading: Romans 8:14,17,19,21,23,29; Galatians 4:5-7;
Ephesians 1:5-6; Hebrews 1:1-2; 3:6-8,14-15;
5:8-14; 12:5-7,9,11.

Continuing our contemplation of the spiritual house, we are now to consider the matter of the School of sonship unto adoption. I hesitate to go over the ground of technical differences in terms because that has been done so often, but you will suffer just the briefest word in that connection, as it may be necessary for some.

THE DIVINE CONCEPTION OF "ADOPTION"

When we come to the things of God, we find that we have to change some of our human ideas, and amongst the many things in which that is so there is this matter of adoption. God's idea about adoption is altogether different from ours. Our idea is that of bringing someone into the family from outside, but that is not God's idea at all about adoption. The word "adoption" literally means "the placing of sons," and you will have recognized, if you were following closely, that adoption comes at the close of things in all those passages of Scripture. It is something which lies ahead. We, who have received the Spirit, wait, groaningly wait, for our adoption. We were foreordained unto adoption as sons. It is something for which we are waiting, according to the Word of God. Thus it is not just the matter of bringing into the family, but it is something which is the result of what has transpired since we came into the family, the result of God's dealings with us as being in His family, and you know quite well that different words are used.

The Revised Version is of peculiar value in this connection. The distinction is made quite clear there that, as children of God, we are such on the ground of birth, whilst we are but sons potentially by that birth. We are actually sons, according to that Divine thought as represented in the word "adoption," after we have been in the family for a time and God has dealt with us. Sonship, in the Divine sense, is something which is being developed in us. To be a child is a question of generation; "child" is a generic term, but sonship is something received, something given, something imparted. That is something more than being born.

THE SCRIPTURAL UNFOLDING OF THE SUBJECT

This word, as you have recognized, is used in different ways in the Scripture. In Romans and Galatians, for instance, we have some light upon sonship. It is seen to have its genesis in a basic relationship with God through our receiving the Spirit. We have received the Spirit, and are called sons because we have received the Spirit: but both in the case of Romans and

Galatians the object of those letters was to obviate the grave peril which had come amongst believers of stopping short at a certain point in their spiritual life as born-again ones and not going on to perfection. Their peril was that of being turned aside by the work of the Judaisers, who were coming in to try to arrest the spiritual progress of these believers and bringing in the law again and the Jewish system.

We may indicate here at once that the enemy always withstands very fiercely this matter of spiritual progress unto adoption. The most perilous thing to the enemy is "the adoption of sons." That is the end for him and he knows very well the significance for himself of the Lord's people going on with the Lord unto adoption. These Judaisers were the Devil's instruments to prevent the going on of these people to that glorious end.

So the Holy Spirit, through the Apostle, in these two letters, brings in the light of sonship; that is, he gives the knowledge of sonship in its fuller meaning, and says that basically, by having received the Holy Spirit, we are sons, but that sonship is not realized now in its full meaning and value. That is something unto which we are to go on, in which we are to continue; for the whole creation is waiting, groaning and waiting, for the literal consummation of that which is potential in our having received the Spirit, namely, "the manifestation of the sons of God." When that day comes, the creation will be delivered from its bondage of corruption. But against that deliverance the powers of evil work, and they worked through Judaisers as well as through many other things and people to prevent that glorious deliverance of the creation in the manifestation of the sons of God. So that what we have in Romans and Galatians is light about sonship, the basis of sonship established, but nothing said which carries with it the definite declaration that we have reached all that sonship means. Even in this word, "As many as are led by the Spirit of God, these are sons of God" (A.S.V.), there is no saying that every Christian is a son of God; for is every Christian led by the Spirit of God? It is a spiritual position that is bound up with sonship in God's thought.

Of course, in our birth as children of God, in which sonship is implicit and adoption is prospective, the inheritance is in view, for every one born into this family is a potential heir. If we are children, we are heirs. But it is quite well known that we can be minors while we are heirs, and that is brought out in Galatians. While we may be born heirs, we are still minors, and we cannot have the inheritance until we reach our majority. That is adoption—reaching the majority, coming to full growth, to full manhood.

FULL SONSHIP A CORPORATE MATTER AND GREATLY WITHSTOOD

So that we are brought face to face with this matter of reaching adoption by the development of sonship in us in the School of God. I think I ought to say here that, while this does become an individual and personal matter and must be that in its application, the matter of adoption is one with that of election, and that it is the Church which is in view, not the individual. It is the Church which is the elect body, and it is the Church which is the elect "son," in the sense in which we are speaking of sonship now; and it is the Church which is foreordained unto adoption of sons, not individuals as such, although it has its individual application, and it will be with the manifestation of the sons in the corporate sense, the Church, that God reaches His full end. I say that, because I feel that this matter of sonship involves the truth of the Body of Christ in a very real way. In reality, it depends upon that truth. Now, you may not grasp what I mean. I mean that sonship requires the Body of Christ, is involved in that truth of the Body of Christ, and it is in our relatedness in Christ as fellow-heirs that we shall be developed, that we shall come to fulness, to God's full end. You and I cannot inherit singly, individually: we can only inherit in a related way.

I think that truth goes further than I am now intending to indicate; but let us recognize that the enemy has something very much in view in keeping the light of the Body of Christ from the Lord's people. The reason for that, you see, is on account of our being foreordained unto adoption as sons by Jesus Christ unto Himself, and all that it means to the enemy; for to him it means everything. He loses his place, he loses his kingdom, he loses his title, he loses everything, when this "Corporate Son" is manifested in glory, when this work is completed in the Church and it is found in the throne. It is therefore up to him to keep the light of the Body of Christ from believers: and it is for this reason that, when the Apostle has been led to make the declaration of the truth, "foreordained unto adoption as sons," he gets on his knees, so to speak, and prays:

> *That the God of our Lord Jesus Christ, the Father of*
> *glory, may give unto you a spirit of wisdom and*
> *revelation in the knowledge of him; having the eyes*
> *of your heart enlightened, that ye may know what*
> *is the hope of his calling, what the riches of the*
> *glory of his inheritance in the saints...*
> (Ephesians 1:17-18, A.S.V.).

It is fervent prayer against this blinding, darkening, withholding work of the adversary as to the light concerning the
Church's nature, calling and destiny. You will agree with me
that there are comparatively few Christians, when you go over
the whole range of Christians to-day in all the world, comparatively few who have light, the revelation of the Body of
Christ; and that represents a most disastrous result of Satanic
activity, the blinding of the saints. Oh no, this is not some truth
which is an optional thing. This is something which is bound
up with the very purpose of God and the undoing of all
Satanic work.

Well, Romans 8 is a tremendous chapter along many lines,
but that great summing up is immense. The creation, subjected to vanity, is seen groaning and travailing unto the manifestation of the sons of God, when it will be delivered from the
bondage of corruption: and then, unto that, the elect instrument is shown—"Whom he foreknew, he also foreordained to
be conformed to the image of his Son" (A.S.V.). It is the Church
being brought in and it is a thing of immense importance, and
it is necessary to see that, before we can appreciate this training of sons unto adoption.

We are in a school for a tremendous destiny. We are in the
school which has as its end something of such significance
and importance that we can scarce imagine; and so we have
not to regard lightly the child-training of the Lord. Oh, again
our human ideas must not be brought into the Divine realm
when we use the word "chastening." What a poor translation!
Even the Revisers have not helped us very much. It is simply
"child-training." I think that, as a youngster, that chapter in
Hebrews was my pet aversion in the Bible when I heard it
read! My whole being rose up against that. I suppose that is

quite natural; but if only we had been given the two words instead of that deplorable word "chastening." It might at least have taken the edge off things. "My son, despise not thou the child-training of the Lord." There is something better about that. "Whom the Lord loveth, He trains," He child-trains.

Well, we come to the business of child-training right away. Here, in this fifth chapter of the Hebrew letter, we have these school features mentioned in various words, as you notice.

> *Though he were a Son, yet learned he obedience*
> *by the things which he suffered.*

That is a school verse.

> *When by reason of the time ye ought to be*
> *teachers... (A.S.V.).*

It is another school verse.

> *Every one that partaketh of milk is without*
> *experience... (A.S.V.).*

That is a school verse.

> *...by reason of use have their senses exercised....*

That is what happens at school. Here we are found right in the School of sonship.

THE PRACTICAL DIFFERENCE BETWEEN "CHILDREN" AND "SONS"

Now, in the practical way, let us note the difference between infants, spiritually, called children in the New Testament, and sons. The difference is simply this, that infants or children have everything done for them and they live in the good of that for which they themselves have had no exercise. That is the difference. An infant is one who lives on the good of other people's exercise and has never had any exercise for itself. Everything has been done and prepared for it. Everything is coming to it as from the outside, and nothing has been done by the child itself. I think that is the main mark of an infant. But a son, in the spiritual and scriptural sense, is one who is in the way of having the root of the matter in himself, who is progressively coming out of the realm where everything is done for him and where he has no exercise at all about things, to the place where it is going on in him and he is becoming one who is competent in himself, and no longer dependent upon what others do and say. Everything is not being brought ready made to him. There is a sense in which it is being made in him and he is making it in his own experience by the exercise of his own senses. That is the main difference, spiritually, between an infant or child, and a son.

These two words here are very helpful words—"senses exercised." As children of God, we are regarded as having spiritual senses, and the object of God's dealings with us in His child-training is to bring those senses into exercise, so that by that exercise we may have experience: and what a tremendous thing is experience, and of what value. They are the people who count, these who have experience, and experience comes through the exercise of the senses.

But there are a great many people who never graduate from spiritual childhood and infancy to sonship; and why is it? You see, God does not sovereignly and by determination make sons of us. Oh no, God is not going to make sons of everybody on His own initiative, by His own power. We have a place in this. The responsibility, as you notice, in every one of these Scriptures, is thrown back upon believers themselves, and it is made very clear in very strong words, that the responsibility does rest upon them. The bringing up so frequently of those words relating to Israel's downfall in the wilderness shows what responsibility rests upon the children of God in this matter.

> To-day if ye shall hear his voice, harden not your
> hearts, as in the provocation
> (Hebrews 3:15, A.S.V.).

That has usually been used as a text for a Gospel address to unbelievers; but in the New Testament, it was never used in that way. It may be legitimate, but it was never used in that way in the New Testament. It was always used for Christians, for believers, as a warning, and to bring home to believers this matter of responsibility, of something resting with us.

PURPOSEFULNESS A REQUIREMENT IN WOULD-BE SONS

Now, that means there is something basic to sonship unto adoption, and that is a purposefulness to go on with God. There must be about us this sense of purpose, this factor and feature of purpose, purposefulness to go on with God, and the Lord calls for that. Oh, the New Testament might be said to be one continuous urge to that, an urge to be characterized by a spiritual purpose, of meaning to go on, and it is upon that the Lord operates. Now I say that to lead to this. It is just that very purposefulness of heart which brings us into all the trouble. Perhaps if we recognized what that means, it would be as helpful a thing as could be said to us. The people who are not characterized by that spirit of purpose and are just content to be little babes all their lives and to have everything done for them and dished up to them and who never have any exercise for themselves, usually have a fairly comfortable time. They are fairly satisfied and pleased with life and they do not want anything else. But let a man become marked by this sense of earnest purpose, and it will not be long before he is in trouble! If you mean to go on, then you have come out of the nursery into the school, and the nature of this school is a very difficult one.

THE DISCIPLINE THAT MAKES ALL INWARD AND LIVING

It just means this, that God is going to put and precipitate us into the most difficult situations. A situation is only difficult if you cannot cope with it. If you find the thing altogether beyond your measure; your measure of strength, your measure of wisdom, your measure of knowledge, then you are in difficulty: and that is the sort of thing the Lord does with people who mean business with Him. He puts them into difficult situations, and His whole object is to get their spiritual senses exercised, so that they may gain experience, may have the root of the matter in themselves. Thus all our nice, comfortable line of things falls away at once and we find ourselves in a realm with which we cannot cope, for which we are not sufficient. We have been in the habit of asking questions and getting them answered; now, no one can answer our questions, no answer comes from the outside.

Of course, people can say things to us and we may get a measure of help from those who have experience; but God is going to shut us up to the fact that it has to become ours by experience and in truth. It does not matter what anyone else says, we know quite well that we have to prove that for ourselves; they cannot lift us out of our difficulty. We constantly revert to the old childish way of running around asking somebody to solve our problems, but we have to come out of that. That is not going to work any longer. Really, deep down in us, we know that it does not work. We are not getting what we are after. We know now we have not to have something said to us, but something done in us. We have to be brought ourselves to a position, not to a mental solution; and if you are all the time trying to get intellectual solutions to your spiritual problems, you are still in the nursery.

If you are going really to come through to God's full and intended end, you have to know the Lord for yourself in an inward way, and unto that it may be necessary for the Lord to suspend all external helps and render all others incapable of coming to your rescue, flinging you wholly back upon Himself; to prove Him, to know Him, to be deeply, deeply exercised in your own spirit. That exercise enlarges capacity, and enlarged capacity means enlarged impartation from the Lord. That is the School of sonship unto adoption.

You see, spirituality, which is the nature of sonship, is not mental at all. That is to say, it is not a matter of having all our mental problems answered for us by somebody who has an answer to give us. You can never reach spirituality philosoph- ically, logically, academically. You may go all over the world and get many questions answered, but that does not mean that you have come into spiritual enlargement. No, that is a very small realm, after all. Most of us have been there. We know quite well it never got us anywhere at all; and what a time we had and how disappointed we were!

In my own experience in that realm, where it was all a mat- ter of getting answers to spiritual problems, or trying to get them, along intellectual lines, with a very wide search for sat- isfaction of mind and heart along that line, I reached a point that Robert Browning (a very much bigger man than I am) reached, as the goal of all his enquiry along that line, namely, that it is as difficult not to believe in God as to believe in Him. Well, how far does that get you? But that is the boundary of all inquiry philosophically! You may have decided not to believe anything about God; then there is a sunset and all your decisions are tested at once. You have to say, Man never made that; where did it come from? and you are back to your old questions.

The Lord Jesus Christ says, "If any man willeth to do his will, he shall know of the teaching" (John 7:17, A.S.V.). That is only the Gospel way of putting in germ form this great truth of sonship, namely, that you know by experience and not by intellectual inquiry and by people telling you from the outside. You do not come into anything by that way, for what logic can build up, logic can pull down. No, God dealeth with us as with—what? Students in the academic sense? No, as with sons. And where do we locate sonship? God is the Father of our spirits; therefore our spirits are the seat of sonship and all His dealings are with our spirits. Thus it is a matter of spiritual growth, spiritual enlargement: that is growth in sonship unto adoption. Oh yes, it is experience.

A FINAL EMPHASIS AND EXHORTATION

Now, I wonder if you have grasped what I have been saying and are going to be helped by it; that, so soon as you mean business with God, you have put yourself in the way of numerous difficulties and all that has been so wonderful to you is going to fall away: all that has been your satisfaction is probably going for a time to cease to be that, and you are coming into a realm where you have to find God in a new way, in a manner in which you have never hitherto known Him, and where you can no longer really get help from the outside; I mean final help. You may just be helped, but the Lord does not allow those ready-made things to come and put you into the position to which He is leading you. You have to get there for yourself.

You may be helped as to how to get there, and as to what is God's goal for you, and as to how other people came through to that end; but no one now from the outside can do it for you and you know that God has shut you up to have this thing done in you and it is solely a matter between you and the Lord in your spiritual history. You may be right in the midst of the most mature Christians who have gone that way and who know and you may be as one alone. You know you do not know as they know; but do not despair. If you are marked by this spirit of purposefulness with God, that means He has you in His school, and it is a good indication when you begin to get real deep spiritual exercise.

We have all met those people who have lived on the basis of spiritual infancy all their lives, and they can never help us at all in our deepest need. Indeed, everything was so cut and dried with them they would not investigate anything deeper. They regarded anything deeper as quite superfluous and were quite satisfied and had a kind of answer to everything. But in our heart need they could not touch us at all. We have all been that way.

There was an hour in my own experience when I was there, after years of seeking that answer to a deep sense of need; and, not getting it, I began to go the round to try to see if someone could help me, and I went some hundreds of miles to visit a man who was outstanding as a religious teacher, as a

Bible teacher, and as a name in Christianity. I went to see him to get spiritual help; I was in desperate need, and it was a spiritual situation; and when I put my case before him and told him of my sense of need of a new knowledge of the Lord, he said, "Oh, Sparks, the trouble with you is that you are a bit overtired. You had better go and play golf." He could not understand, could not enter into the situation. I know now why he could not help me and why I got help from no one during that terrible period. I know that God was shutting me up to Himself. I had to come to the place where I could really be a help to others in their hour of need, at least point the way because I had come the way, explaining what God was doing because I had had an experience of His dealings. In order to be of any use at all to those who are going to be sons, to have a ministry for the sons of God, a ministry which, though so imperfectly, so inadequately, touches that great end of adoption; in order to have the smallest part in such a ministry, God has had to shut us up to Himself so that no one could help us.

Do not take that wrongly. Do not take that to mean that you are to cut yourself off from fellowship and from all help that may be available. That would be a misapprehension of what I am saying, and might make things infinitely more difficult and put you in a false position. But I am saying that in your heart of hearts you will find, while there may be help given to you by ministries, fellowship, advice, counsel, by explanation, the real thing has to be born and developed in your own self. You have to have the root of the matter in you and no one can bring that about but the Lord Himself by His own dealings with you.

So you will be plunged into darkness. I do not mean the darkness of being out of union with God, the darkness of lost assurance of salvation; but you will be plunged into darkness in experience in order to make new discoveries, in order that the Lord may give you light through exercise. God dealeth with you as with—not bricks, but living stones, sons. That is an honor, that is a great thing, that ought to inspire us. If we have boys, they always feel tremendously encouraged if we put our hand on their shoulder and say, "Now, old boy...," and begin to talk to them as responsible persons, not just dealing with them all the time as babes. My son, I want you to do this for me; I want you to take this bit of responsibility; I want you to look after things for me while I am away. Then something rises up and there is a reach out to be what father wants.

Now, in a sense, that is what God is doing. He is saying, I do not want you to be babes always, I want to put responsibility upon you; I have some big things for you to do. Now, come along! He may put us into some very difficult situation, but the very sense of being called to the responsibility will make us seek to know how to meet this situation. A man flung into the sea to learn to swim learns far better than the man who has the doctrine about swimming. The Lord does that in love; but He does it. Whom the Lord loveth He child-trains.

I wonder how many of us would be very pleased if our parents had always done things for us, always sheltered us from having the trouble, the bother, the worry, the necessity of doing things or finding out how to do them for ourselves. I am quite sure none of us would think that was love in our parents. I think we would come to a time when we would say, I have nothing good to say of my parents; they have landed me into very, very great difficulty by their false idea of love. Here I am;

everybody knows I am no good, and I know it myself! But "whom the Lord loveth, He child-trains."

Look ahead to see all that is going to be. You see, there is a throne in view, there is government in view. I do not know how men manage in the governments of this world. It seems to me that they are able to pass from one department to another in the State. I do not know how that is done, but I do not believe that it is because it is in them. So much is a matter of routine, of form. It can be taken up as something already highly organized and arranged. Of course, I would not say of all statesmen that it was not in them, but I am speaking generally. Now, the Lord is having no official appointments in the great administration of His Kingdom. He is going to have people who have had quality wrought in them. It is unto that the Church, the Body of Christ, is called, and it has to be in us. That is no child's play. That is a thing for full-grown men.

If that is not true, then I do not understand the teaching of the New Testament about going on to full growth, nor do I understand the Lord's dealings with His Church. If all that matters is just that we should be born again, have forgiveness of sins, and go to Heaven, why all this in the Bible and in our experience? It is certainly not for something here. There may be values here, but they are not commensurate with what we have to go through. It is just at the time when we are beginning to get mature and are a little use to the Lord that He takes us away. We cannot pass it on. There may be some fruit, some value of it here, but not at all commensurate with all this training. No, it is for some other purpose. We say "Higher Service." Well yes, that is what it is.

The Lord give us grace then to endure chastening as sons, so that He may have that company upon which He can place the great responsibility which it is His will to give.

CHAPTER SEVEN

GRADUATION FROM THE SCHOOL OF SONSHIP

Reading: Romans 8:19, 21-23; Hebrews 1:2; 2:5-8,9-11; 3:1,7-8; 12:5-6; Revelation 12:5

In our previous meditation, we were occupied with the School of sonship unto adoption. We are now going to follow that on to the next stage.

We were seeing a little of the nature, meaning and need for transition from spiritual infancy to the School of sonship. A very real experience is that transition and a very deep one for those who enter into it. A whole new set of conditions perfectly strange to us is connected with that further movement in the life of the child of God which marks the passage from spiritual childhood to spiritual sonship, or the School of sonship.

I suppose most of us remember when we went to a new school, or when we went to school for the first time. Everything was strange, everything was new. We had to take up things from the very first point. It was an entirely new world: and so it is in the life of the child of God. It is an entirely new world, a new set of conditions, something with which we are altogether unfamiliar when that point is reached where God takes us in hand to see that we are no longer children, but are brought into the School of sonship with adoption in view; adoption, of course, according to the Divine meaning of that word, not our natural meaning.

THE PURPOSE OF OUR GRADUATION AS SONS

Now we are going for a little while to consider the graduation from the School of sonship, graduating to that for which school has been going on, all that child-training which, as the Lord Himself knows and let us know that He knows, is for the present not joyous but grievous. But there is the graduation day.

The whole creation waits for that graduation day with bated breath and an inward yearning, the day of the manifestation of the sons of God, the *placing* of sons to which we referred in our previous meditation, which is the meaning of the word "adoption"; not bringing into the family, but the placing of sons who have qualified through the school. And what is the graduation of sonship, unto what is it? It is unto the Throne.

> *Not unto angels* [not unto angels of any rank, not
> even the highest rank of archangels] *did he subject
> the world to come, whereof we speak. But one hath
> somewhere testified, saying, What is man, that
> thou art mindful of him? Or the son of man, that
> thou* [settest him apart]? (A.S.V.)

That is the true rendering of the latter sentence; not "visitest him" as we commonly use the word, but "settest him apart";

that man, in a word, is in view with God from eternity for this purpose, to have the throne, the government, the dominion over the world to come in union with God's Son, as the sons brought by that Son to glory.

There is the Heir in Hebrews 1:2—"...whom he hath appointed heir of all things...." There are the heirs in chapter 2—"...bringing many sons unto glory...."

The throne is that which is in view at the end of school, the graduation, and it is that which is referred to in Revelation 12. The governing principle of Revelation 12 is sonship brought out to completion, a man child.

> *She was delivered of a son, a man child, who is to rule all the nations with a rod of iron* [This is sonship]: *and her child was caught up unto God, and unto his throne"* (A.S.V.).

That is the graduation.

THE MAN CHILD OF REVELATION 12

Now, I am going to stay for the miserable business of getting rid of a few misconceptions about this chapter. The accepted and firmly held view concerning this chapter is, that this woman is Israel and that this man child is Christ. I will not impute motives and reasons to the holders of that view, but it does seem to me that only a prejudiced mind could hold it, a mind not willing to accept what is, I think, quite patently the truth.

This Book of Revelation begins with a pronouncement from Heaven that what is going to be shown is "things which must shortly come to pass," and that pronouncement was made years and years after Christ had gone to Heaven. It was future. Moreover, when Christ went to Heaven, Satan was not cast out of Heaven as is the case in Revelation 12; for, nearly forty years after Christ went to Heaven, Paul wrote his letter to the Ephesians, and in chapter 6 we have this revelation of the nature and sphere of the Church's warfare: "Our wrestling is not against flesh and blood, but against the principalities, against the powers, against the world-rulers of this darkness, against the spiritual hosts of wickedness in the heavenly places" (A.S.V.). Satan was not deposed when Christ was caught up to the throne. Thirdly, the dragon was not cheated of his prey in the case of the Lord Jesus. The Lord Jesus was slain by the dragon, and it is a part of the great and glorious truth that it was through death that He destroyed him that had the power of death, namely, the Devil. Satan, the dragon, thought he had swallowed up Christ perhaps, but he discovered that he had been swallowed up. But the Lord Jesus did not escape the great red dragon by a rapture; not at all. The dragon got him so far and slew him. But therein is the glorious sovereignty of God, and that is another line of truth altogether: God's sovereignty wrought in the very presence of Satan's triumph. But that is not this.

Then this woman is a paradox, a contradiction. She is at one and the same time in Heaven clothed in glory and on the earth clothed with trouble and travail. She is clothed with the sun in Heaven, and yet in the next breath she is travailing on the earth. Is not that just exactly what we have in the letter to the Ephesians about the Church? In the heavenlies, in Christ Jesus blessed with every spiritual blessing, and yet at the same time the letter shows us very clearly right at the heart of it that the Church is down here and in conflict.

She has an earthly walk and is meeting things down here while at the same time in the heavenlies. A contradiction apparently: at one and the same time in Heaven glorious and yet on earth in tribulation. That is the Church. Well, is not that enough, though there is a lot more here?

I know there is another interpretation; that this was not only Israel but Christ Himself, and that we are the seed of Christ. But that is only just allowed to go so far. It does not carry us through satisfactorily. But this is the main position held about Israel and Christ, and I say I do not see how it can hold water in the light of even the two or three things that we have just noted.

You see, you have a correspondence here. In Revelation 2:26-27a you have these very words addressed to the over-comers in the church at Thyatira—"He that overcometh...to him will I give authority over the nations: and he shall rule them with a rod of iron" (A.S.V.). Then in a letter to the church in Laodicea we have these further words: "He that overcometh, I will give to him to sit down with me in my throne, as I also overcame, and sat down with my Father in his throne" (A.S.V.). There is the throne for overcomers and the rule of the nations. Then those very words are reiterated in chapter 12 about the man child caught up to the throne to rule the nation with a rod of iron. And I do not see that we can divorce those words from Hebrews 2—Thou madest him (man) in order to have (that is the sense of the word) dominion over the works of thy hands. Of course there is the union between Christ and His own; that is what Hebrews is speaking about. "Christ as a son over [God's] house; whose house are we...."

So then, having said that much—and I think it is enough, I am not dealing with all the data and points in this chapter—having said that much, we want to come right to our point in this meditation.

The graduation from the School of sonship is to the throne, and it is that throne, with what it means with regard to vocation, to service, to purpose in relation to God's eternal intention, that is in view while God is dealing with us, when God takes us out of the comfortable, pleasant time of spiritual infancy and childhood, where everything is done for us, and puts us into that experience where the thing has to be wrought in us and where, through this deep exercise of our spiritual faculties or senses, we become spiritually responsible sons of God. It is with this in view that God deals with us as with sons. Now, do grasp the meaning of that, what it implies. It implies one or two rather important things.

SPIRITUAL INCREASE RELATED TO THE THRONE AND THE GLORY OF THE LORD

Firstly, it does mean that the deepening of spiritual life, as it is called, or any other terms used for the same thing, is not a matter which is just to issue in our fuller blessing. So often people will bring it right down there to that level of fuller blessing, and we are very often tempted even there, in the time of fire and adversity, to react to this whole thing by saying, Well, if I have Heaven, why need I trouble about all this, and why should I go through all this? Here are plenty of people just very happy and contented; they are saved and they know they are saved, and here am I who have sought to go on with God, and I am having the most awful time. It seems to me that I have got the worst of the bargain, by wanting to go right on with God!

If we look at it like that, purely from the personal point of view of blessing, we have missed our way, and we shall get into difficulties; because, as we have always sought to point out, when you come out of this spiritual infancy into the School of sonship, you graduate from what is personal as to your own interest and blessing into what is for the Lord and not for you. From that time forward the whole motive is, not what I am going to get, but what God is going to get. That is Ephesians. "That ye may know what is...the riches of the glory of *his* inheritance in the saints." Not what I am going to get now: that will follow, that will be all right, the Lord will be faithful; but it is something else.

We have come into the school on the basis of God's eternal purpose, and God's eternal purpose does not begin and end when He has got us born again. God's eternal purpose is only reached when He has got us in the throne. Thus it is the Lord, for the Lord, and what the Lord is after that is the one consideration. It will be glory for me, but that is not the motive of it now. It is this great purpose with which we are called; that is what is governing everything, and it is in the terms of the throne.

So the transition from infancy to the School of sonship, being a very painful thing, and fraught with all sorts of difficulties, brings us nevertheless into relation with that which has been in God's mind from before the world was where we are concerned. Chosen in Christ Jesus "that we should be to the praise of *his* glory." All the dealings of the Lord with us in this school have that throne in view.

WORLD DOMINION THE PRESSING ISSUE OF THE HOUR

What I want to say with special emphasis now is that this matter, as I see and feel it—and I leave it to you to judge whether there is any truth in this—is most fitting in relation to what is happening in the world to-day. It does seem to me that this is a time when this issue is put in a way in which it has never been put before; that is, the issue of the dominion of this world, the issue of Antichrist, is so patent. It is the control and domination of this inhabited earth, and everything connected with this fresh drive to that end is to set aside God and His Christ. It is an evil thing, and it does not need a spiritually minded preacher of the truth to discern that; for many of our leaders of the State to-day have seen it and are using these words. How far they see, we do not know. But they are seeing that all that Christianity stands for is at stake. They are saying, This is a Satanic thing! And they are using the very phrase—Antichrist. It is discerned by men as to what the nature of things is, and we are able, in a special way as enlightened by the Lord, to see what the end of this is. It is the most far-reaching and terrible bid for the throne of this world that has been known. That is what lies behind it and that is what is in view.

Therefore I say that this word is most fit for a time like this, and I am asking myself and I ask you prayerfully to consider whether there must not come something in the nature of a summons to the people of God to recognize this fact, with reference to their calling, namely, that they have to get behind that which is behind the present situation, and that the saints must take the kingdom spiritually now, in a spiritual way, in order that they may come to the place of the throne for the age to come.

We here perhaps—though let us not think too highly of our-selves, more highly than we ought to think—but it may be that our little gathering here with all its earthly insignificance has yet a significance which is very far reaching, seeing that we are here in the audience chamber of God concerning this great matter of the dominion of this world. In a small way, it affects us very seriously. I ask you to pray about this, very earnestly and continually that there might be a movement of God's Spirit within the circle of His own people in a new way, to produce this man child that overcomes and takes the throne. It is quite clear, from Revelation 2 and 3, that all do not come to that position, and equally so from all these exhortations and warn-ings about Israel missing the goal in the wilderness, falling by the way, as warnings to the Church to beware of the same calamity. "To-day if ye shall hear his voice, harden not your hearts" (A.S.V.). I wonder if any of us have a hardened heart, not against the Lord in a general way, but against this.

You harden by using special terms. Oh, how people have sought to close the door by sticking labels on! Get rid of terms. Call it Selective Rapture if you like; I do not call it that. Call it Overcomer Testimony, if you like. It makes little differ-ence, if you mean by that, That is an interpretation, that is a peculiar teaching! Well, that is a hardening of the heart. What if this should happen to be true! We have to look this thing square in the eyes. Is there any possibility that this is true? If there is, it is a tremendous thing; the biggest issue in the his-tory of this world is bound up with it, nothing less than the dominion, the throne. I suggest to you that there is a good deal to-day which would lead us to open the door of possi-bilities, to suppositions.

AN OBJECT LESSON AND THE NEED FOR
OPEN-HEARTED INQUIRY

You know certain nations at our own door are suffering untold misery, because as long as seven years ago they were told of secret propaganda going on within the borders of their own country, and working its way secretly and subtly into high places, but would not believe it. They were told what that was going to end in, what the object was, what the result would be, and they said, No, impossible! I ask you this: If nine months ago a prophet had stood up in some prominent place in this world and prophesied the history of the following nine months, what would have happened to him? Seven or eight countries overrun and surprised, and this final terrible collapse of France! He would have been put in a lunatic asylum or have been lynched, he would have been shut up for safety. But it has happened: the unbelievable has happened and is happening. No one would believe it or accept it. See how they are suffering for saying, Impossible! Ridiculous!

Ah, I say to you that this should be a lesson to us. That is a trick of Satan. It is a part of his strategy, to work subtly and at the same time to make people believe there is nothing, that all is well; to be working underneath to the internal disintegration and downfall of a people, and yet on the surface to be making nice speeches. This is a Satanic method, and again and again Satan has gained his strategical advantage by that same means. And I say to you that at least we ought to come to a thing like this and say, Well, it is just possible that may be right, and if there is the remotest possibility of its being right, it is such a big thing we had better attend to it! I know many have managed to get past that, but I say again, from the lowest level of making this appeal, that it just may be that the

Lord's Word is true after all. It just may be that this is the true revelation of God's thought and intention; that He chose an elect people, a company that has come to be called the Church, He chose that company, that Body, that corporate entity in Christ before the world was, with a view to it coming through at length to take the throne as His vessel and instrument for governing His universe. I say, that may be true. All I ask you to do is to consider the possibility of its being true, and if only you will allow that, it will give you real pause: and then to see that this is quite true so far as the Scripture and the experience of the Lord's people are concerned in a spiritual way. God is doing a certain thing in His people, in many at least who are pressing on with Him, those of whom we were speaking in our previous meditation who are marked by a purposefulness with God.

In these He begins to do something deep and strange and painful, the end of which is never, never reached in this earthly life, the value of which is never entered into by anybody during their time here on earth. It is unto something: it is the preparation of sons unto adoption to take the throne; and I urge you to pray with regard to your own place in this, and to pray for a movement of God's Spirit within the compass of His people to produce this man child. The Church, as a whole, is moving steadily into this travail.

Then will you not pray that the Lord's people may be enlightened on this matter, enlightened as to what the issue is. It is between Christ and Antichrist, between the Church which is Christ's Body and the whole Antichrist system; for it is quite clear that Antichrist, though he may be an individual opposed to Christ personally, is also a church, a system, a terrible system. Satan has his church opposed to Christ's Church. Blessed be God, we have this assurance, "I will build my church; and the gates of hell shall not prevail against it"!

THE EXPLANATION OF THE MYSTIFYING AND PAINFUL PREPARATION

Well then, that is the matter before us in this School of sonship, namely, the throne. My dear friends, I want to get hold of that in my own heart, and I want you to get hold of it. You see, we are so prone to make our sojourn on this earth the big thing; I mean in the matter of what we are able to do, how much we can do and realize and see in our lifetime, and when we find the Lord shutting us up and limiting us and seeming to put us in prison, ofttimes under the strain and pressure of it, when the iron enters into our soul as with Joseph, we begin to think we have missed the way. Life is going, and it is all unfruitful; we are not doing anything. It is other people who are doing the thing, we are not. Thus we make so much of this present life in the matter of what we are able to do, as though that were everything, whereas (and this, of course, is no argument why we should be slack about doing) so often the Lord has got His greatest effectiveness in those who have been just shut right up, unable to do anything outside.

Is not that the truth about Paul himself? Oh yes, it is, and Paul, as we have often pointed out, was the embodiment of the revelation which was given to him of the dispensation of the Church, and when we come to the end of his life, we have Paul, who had had such a wide scope of ministry, who had been able to do so much, we have this man, with all the values that are in him, put into prison. But we get the concentrated essence of value from those prison experiences. We get the letter to the Ephesians, and that was worth Paul's going to prison, and anything like that will be worth all that we undergo in the School of sonship, which sees a very great deal of what is here on the earth closed down, if only the heavenly may become the far more real and valuable as an expression in us and through us.

But I say I want this to get into my heart, into your hearts, that the Lord is not so much concerned—please do not misunderstand me—the Lord is not so much concerned with how much we do now in this life. He is more concerned with the measure of Christ to which He can bring us in this life..."till we all attain unto the...measure of the stature of the fulness of Christ" (Ephesians 4:13, A.S.V.). It will be Christ corporate who will come to take the kingdom of this world in the coming ages, and it is unto that—the fulness of Christ—that God is working preeminently in our experience, and that is the thing that matters most. It is the most difficult thing for us to accept; a supremely difficult thing for any active temperament to accept. To some it is martyrdom not to be doing something. It may be God's way of getting the enlargement of His Son in His members, the patience of Jesus Christ, among other things.

God has this great thing in view. The issue comes up acutely and in an intensified form as we get near to the great end. In order to answer Satan, to have His answer in a corporate Man, God has to prepare you and me and a company of His people to take the throne, to be caught up unto God and to His throne, to rule the nations with a rod of iron. That, of course, has reference to to-morrow, the to-morrow of the ages I mean, and there is something beyond that, namely, our reigning with Him forever and ever, another form of reigning. I aspire rather to the day after to-morrow than to to-morrow. Ruling with a rod of iron may appeal to us naturally, but we would sooner have the glorious reign where nothing wants a rod of iron. "Now unto him...be the glory in the church and in Christ Jesus unto all generations [of the age of the ages]" (Ephesians 3:20-21, A.S.V.).

It is a big thing for which we go to school for a few years and suffer as we are suffering. It is easy to say that, but it is a painful thing, this school. The Lord knows what He is doing with us. It is the matter of this overcoming, and, in the light of this school or this schooling, we can appreciate the word "overcomer." There is a lot of overcoming to be done. We have to get on top of a very great deal, and the getting on top of many things is leading us to get on top of the Devil and his kingdom. Presently, in the great hour when the sons are manifested, when the man child is caught up to the throne, the creation is to be delivered from the bondage of corruption.

See then the meaning of the day in which we live. See the meaning of the suffering into which we may go yet more deeply, and how it is to be God's answer to this working of Satan that has been going on ever since he made a bid for the place of God's Heir, the Heir of all things. Ever since Satan made that bid and was cast down from the higher to the lower heavens it has been going on, and now it is being brought out in a new way. That is what it is, and you and I, as part of Christ's Body, are called to be God's answer to that, and it is to be so now in a spiritual way. Presently it will be in the full way, the literal way, that the saints will take the kingdom, and He shall come whose right it is to reign. The dominion shall be given unto the saints of the Most High.

CHAPTER EIGHT

"OVER ALL—FAITH,"
AND A FINAL CONSIDERATION

Reading: Ezekiel 43:1-2,4-5,7; Ephesians 1:12; 3:21;
5:25-27; Colossians 1:27; 1 Peter 4:14;
Hebrews 10:37-39; 11:1.

In these meditations, we have been looking at some of the major features of God's spiritual house in which we who are the Lord's are living stones. We have been seeking to see what our being living parts of a spiritual house means, and there are two things which remain for this present time, which we trust the Lord will enable us to say. One is something which governs all these matters, and the other is the final feature of this spiritual house. I put it in that way because I think it will be most helpful to deal with these remaining matters in that order, and the one will lead quite naturally to the other, as you will see.

This thing which governs all the features, the spiritual features, of this spiritual house of God is faith.

FAITH IN RELATION TO

(A) THE EXALTATION OF THE LORD JESUS

The first feature that we considered was that this spiritual house, of which we are a living part if we are in Christ, stands for the setting forth in a living way of the exaltation of the Lord Jesus. We saw how that was the first great note in the Church's history on the day of Pentecost.

> *God hath made him both Lord and Christ, this*
> *Jesus whom ye crucified* (Acts 2:36, A.S.V.).

> *Being...[at] the right hand of God exalted...he hath*
> *poured forth this, which ye see and hear*
> (Acts 2:33, A.S.V.).

It was a glorious expression of, and testimony to, the exaltation of the Lord Jesus, and the Church is constituted for that purpose, to maintain that, not firstly as a part of its doctrine, but as being in itself the living exhibit thereof throughout the dispensation and to hold that testimony in a living way right to the end.

But we shall find that, in that matter, as in all the others, it very soon becomes a question of a living faith. It was not that so much on the day of Pentecost. The Spirit came, and filled them that had believed, baptized them within and without, and in that mighty tidal-wave of the Spirit it was not difficult for them to proclaim and give expression to the exaltation of the Lord Jesus. And that is true in principle, although perhaps not in the same outward way, in the case of every child of God, when they first come into a living union with the Lord Jesus. It is not difficult at that time for us to proclaim, and by our very faces to announce, that Jesus is exalted, Jesus is Lord, Jesus lives. That is our first note of testimony when we receive the Spirit. It is the first thing which expresses itself in a believer. But we all have lived to know that it is not always as easy as that. It does not always come as spontaneously as that. We move into a time when, while the fact remains, we have to hold on to the fact in sheer and grim faith.

We have to answer to apparent contradictions to the fact with an attestation of faith; for things rise up and there is a mighty reaction of the enemy to our testimony and to our position, and we have to hold the position in blind faith; not in feeling faith, not in seeing faith, but in cold, blind faith we have to maintain our position that Jesus is Lord, Jesus is exalted, Jesus is on the throne; and it is only by faith being put forth in the fact that we win through, and that testimony becomes a powerful thing in our deliverance, in our very life.

So faith governs this matter, and we shall find that, as we get nearer to the end, the challenge to the Lordship, the exaltation, the Kingship, the enthronement of the Lord Jesus will become intensely severe. It will be a bitter challenge and there will be a situation in which nothing but just faith, naked faith, on the part of God's elect, will keep them standing in the good of that truth, that Jesus Christ, after all, has the reins of government in His hands. If one thing is true about overcomers who do overcome, it is that they overcome by reason of faith; and faith is faith. So let us not, after all that we have heard and all that in which we have gloried, expect that this is going to be anything other than a testimony in faith. It is not going to be a life of knowing by every evidence, by every proof, by every sign, by every sensation, that Jesus is reigning without any question at all. It is not going to be like that. Do not expect that it is going to be like that. The Word of God makes it very clear that it is not the case. Mark the context, for example, of the verses we read from Hebrews 10. (A.S.V.).

> *For yet a very little while, he that cometh shall come, and shall not tarry. But my righteous one shall live by **faith**.*

(B) MINISTERING UNTO THE LORD

Then we spoke about another feature of this spiritual house, that it is in existence to minister to God's satisfaction and pleasure. That is a very nice idea! It is a very pleasant thought, a very beautiful thing, to think of being in existence to minister to God's pleasure, to God's satisfaction, to God's glory, and perhaps again at the outset we feel it is not such a big proposition. When we are in those first days of the blossom of spiritual experience, we think that the Lord is very well pleased and happy about us, and we are very happy with the Lord, and it is all right, the Lord is getting something. It is not so difficult to think about this matter of ministering to the Lord's good pleasure.

But we discover again that, as the Lord's, we are led out into the wilderness. There is a side of our being which has to be dealt with, that side which has been in the habit of having the upper hand, of having the preeminence, of doing all the dictating and the governing, and that has to be put down and another side, namely, that which is of the Lord, has to be brought up, and we come into that realm of which the Apostle speaks—"The flesh lusteth against the Spirit, and the Spirit against the flesh: [for] these are contrary the one to the other" (Galatians 5:17). There is something going on in us and when we get out there in that wilderness and are in the deep realities of trial, the demand on faith is no light thing. I am thinking of Israel's 40 years in the wilderness while the Lord was dealing with them along the line of discipline, to bring them to that aspect of the Cross as represented by the Jordan, where it is no longer just a matter of their being justified by faith, but of being delivered from themselves by faith: and that required a great exercise of faith when the Jordan overflowed all its banks. But it was in the wilderness, and it is in the wilderness that we, under the hand of the Lord, are brought to understand that no flesh can glory in His presence; that in us, that is, in our flesh, no good thing dwelleth, and we have to have that brought home to us so that it is not just a theory, but a desperate and awful reality. So we cry, "O wretched man that I am!"

At such a time you have great questions as to whether there is any ministry to the glory and pleasure of God. It seems anything but that! And yet, beloved, when we are going through all that under the hand of God, out there in the wilderness, the very fact that we repose faith in the Lord to perfect that which concerneth us, to carry through that which He has commenced unto the day of Jesus Christ, is something that very much ministers to God's pleasure and satisfaction. Just picture it in its figurative setting with Israel in the wilderness. There was the Tabernacle in the midst, and there was God right in that Tabernacle in the Most Holy Place in the Shekinah glory. He was there all the time in the Shekinah glory inside, but on the outside, well, it was a wilderness all right, and there were those horrible ugly covers of the Tabernacle and the glory was hidden. All the beauty was concealed and the outer covers were anything but beautiful and glorious, and the Lord's people were having a very trying time.

But at any moment, in the darkest day, the most difficult hour, when things seemed to be most hopeless, at any moment had you looked inside, the glory was to be found there, and it was just a matter of their faith. If they took the appearances as the criterion, they could say, Oh, we cannot see the Lord; everything looks very uninteresting and anything but glorious, and the situation is a very deplorable one and all this that we are going through and all this lack of sight with regard to the Lord's presence—well, there is nothing in it! We give it up! Again and again in the New Testament, the Lord comes back upon that to warn the Church against such an attitude. "They could not enter in because of unbelief" (Hebrews 3:19). And their unbelief worked in this way, "Is the Lord among us or not?" That was the thing that upset the Lord so much that He refused to allow that generation to go into the land. They asked the ultimate question, Is the Lord among us or not?

> But at any moment, in the darkest day, the most difficult hour, when things seemed to be most hopeless, at any moment had you looked inside, the glory was to be found there, and it was just a matter of their faith.

Why did they ask that? Because of appearances and difficulties. The glory was veiled, and it was only at rare intervals that the glory was displayed. For the greater part, the glory was not seen. Ah, what then of that word, Christ in you, the hope of glory! Now, that is the word the Apostle by the Spirit addresses to the Church, in the Church's time of difficulty, adversity, discipline, trial, of going through things, and he says, in effect, "Ah, yes, that is how it is on the outside, that is how it is in the matter of circumstances, but Christ in you is the hope of glory": and hope that is seen is not hope. Even this is a matter of faith.

We do not always feel Christ in us. We do not live every moment in the consciousness that the Lord is inside; but He is, as truly as the Shekinah glory was there within the Most Holy Place when there was nothing on the outside to evidence it. At any moment you would have been able to prove it could you have looked within. So is it with the Lord's spiritual house, whose house are we. He is there and you have to take an attitude towards this outside situation by which the Lord is bringing us into a new realm, a new position, that, after all, it is not the ultimate thing, the preeminent thing: the Lord Himself has said, "I will never leave thee." Faith laying hold of that when it seems there is nothing whatever that contributes to the Lord's glory and satisfaction in us, faith laying hold of the faithfulness of God and trusting Him to carry His work in us through to perfection, is itself a ministration to God's pleasure.

You see that by the contrary. How displeased God was with that generation. Of them He said, They shall not enter into My rest. Why was He displeased? Because they did not trust Him to get them through. They surrendered to the appearances of things in their own lives.

(C) Ministering to the Life of Others

Then the third thing we spoke about was that the Church is here as a spiritual house for the purpose of ministering to the life of others, of the Lord's people, and here the same principle holds good. It is such a good idea, it is such a fine thought: ministering to the life of others, that is splendid! If only that can be, well, it is a great thing to minister to the life of others, and the very suggestion makes us rise up and feel better. But you remember what the Apostle Paul said: "Death worketh in us, but life in you" (2 Corinthians 4:12). You see, it is Gideon's fleece all over again, wrung out, dried, and all around wet, and our ministering to the life of others is like that very often. We are just as dry as dry bones, wrung out. We are not conscious of being full of life and ministering life to others, and yet it is often just then that others do receive something, and that is to the glory of God. Oh, we said, we never thought there could be any blessing in it! Well, the Lord was not letting our flesh glory in the giving of life to others, but they were getting it.

You see, it is again a matter of faith. Do not think that this ministering to the life of others is always going to be something of which we are conscious, that we are just full and overflowing with life, and people are getting it. I think more often than not it is the other way round. For us it is a grim holding on to God in faith and others are getting the blessing and we are amazed. It can be so. Have faith then; fulfill your ministry in faith.

> He that goeth forth and weepeth, bearing precious
> seed, shall doubtless come again with rejoicing,
> bringing his sheaves with him (Psalm 126:6).

Weeping, but in faith. The reward of faith is a great "doubtless."

(D) A Local Corporate Representation of Christ

Then our fourth feature of the spiritual house was that it is here to be a local corporate representation of the Lord Jesus. We meditated upon that word of His, "Where two or three are gathered together in my name, there am I in the midst of them" (Matthew 18:20), and dwelt upon it as a statement pointing on to the great truth of the Body of Christ, that, wherever there are two or three members of His Body, that is a representation and expression of Christ in that place.

But I again see that so often this is only made good by faith. "Where two or three are gathered together in my name, there am I in the midst"—but faith has to rise up very strongly and very deliberately and lay hold of that. You see, you may be two or three gathered somewhere, but there may be nothing whatever of an expression and manifestation of the presence of Christ. You have to come together in faith. You have to stand together in faith. You have to put your feet squarely upon His assurance and declare yourself as resting upon that assurance, and as we take hold of the truth that where the Body of the Lord is, it is then that the thing becomes a reality. We do not make it a reality by faith, but we bring out the reality by faith. The Lord looks for a definite standing upon these things and an assertion of faith. We are here; yes, but we are not here just as two or three gathered in the name of Jesus in a passive way. There will be no expression of the Lord's presence when things are like that. We come together in faith and we stand in faith that there is going to be an expression of the Lord by our very being here; and, unless we come together like that, it will be but a congregation, a service, a coming and going.

When we come together in a living way with a living faith, it is not an address we have come to listen to, but we have come definitely to meet with the Lord, and the Lord has assured us that, as we are gathered together in His name, we shall meet Him. If that is our spirit, our attitude, there will be something of a living expression of the Lord. Faith is a great factor in the matter of corporate life to make its values real. I cannot go further than that.

(E) TESTIMONY TO THE OVERTHROW OF SATAN

The fifth feature was that this spiritual house is here to testify in a living way to the overthrow of Satan. Well, that is a fact; Satan has been overthrown by Christ. So far as the Lord Jesus is concerned, the overthrow of Satan has been accomplished and established, and on the day of Pentecost there was no difficulty in their believing it, enjoying it and proclaiming it. But they lived to see other days when it was not just like that. They lived to see days when it seemed that Satan was anything but overthrown, anything but disposed. They saw him apparently doing just as he wanted to do, having it all his own way. They saw him bringing to death their fellow-believers and colleagues in ministry. They saw the ravages of the Devil on the right hand and on the left. Does this mean that the thing they once said so strongly and with such conviction is no longer true and they were mistaken even then? Not at all! This matter has to become a matter of the faith of the Lord's people. The overthrow of Satan, so far as this world is concerned, is a matter of the militant faith of the Church.

I simply draw from Ephesians this. When the Apostle has told us of all the armour that we are to put on in this spiritual warfare against the wiles of the Devil, he says, Now above all take the shield of faith. Our English language is poor in expressing what Paul said. Paul did not say "above all" in the sense in which we should mean it. He said, Now *over* all take the big shield of faith. As you know, the Roman legions had more than one kind of shield. They had the little round shield, which was only for the protection of the face and head against arrows and darts. But then they had the big shield, which could shield them completely, and often an army marched into battle with it over them. As they put the big shields side by side, it was like forming a solid mail roof. They marched under it, the big shield being over everything, covering everything.

All else requires this one thing. All else may yield, prove insufficient. With everything, over and above everything—faith! It requires the militant faith of the Church to bring about here what Christ has brought about in Heaven, namely, the overthrow of the Evil One. It is by faith now that Satan is overthrown, so far as the Church is concerned, and so far as things here are concerned. But of course, our faith is not in something which is going to be, it is in something which already is, namely, Christ's victory.

(F) PRESENT TESTIMONY TO THE COMING DAY OF GLORY

Now I come to the last thing, which has not been mentioned. The final feature of this spiritual house, which comes up with the passages we have read, is that the spiritual house, the Church, is here in the light of the coming day of the fulness of Glory, to stand in the light of that, to receive upon itself the light of that, and to reflect the light of that day that is coming.

In Ezekiel's Temple, you notice how we read that, after all those goings in and out and round about and through and up and down, at last the man led him by the way of the gate which is toward the east and toward the glory. The east is the sunrise, the new day, and it is by that way that the fulness of the glory comes in. The house, you see, stands right in the way of the coming glory. It is there with its face toward the sunrise, toward the glory. That is the type in Ezekiel, but we have many other passages.

"We should be unto the praise of his glory" (A.S.V.). That is the Church in Ephesians. But there is this passage in Hebrews.

*For yet a very little while, he that cometh shall
come, and shall not tarry. But my righteous one
shall live by faith....Now faith is assurance of
things hoped for, a conviction of things not seen*
(Hebrews 10:37-38; 11:1, A.S.V.).

Here, you see, is a standing by faith in the light of that glorious hope, that blessed hope, and knowing in the heart the
assurance of that unseen glory. We are here as the Lord's
house to be a present testimony to the coming day of glory.
But that is not testimony in word, in doctrine; it is to be in life,
in reality. But that can only be in a spiritual way, and therefore
it can only be along the line of faith. We have to apprehend
the day of the Lord, the day of glory, the coming of the Lord
in glory; we have to apprehend that in a spiritual way. There
are a lot of people who are apprehending it in a prophetical
way, but I do not always find that the study of prophecy
results in glory. I find very often that it results in a good deal
of death and confusion, and it is not all prophetical students
who are living in the glory of the coming day. They are living
in the belief of it, in the argument about it, but not in the glory
of it. It is no mere doctrinal or mental apprehension of that
great truth that will bring the glory of it into our lives, but a
spiritual apprehension.

I used to study prophecy a good deal, and the Book of the
Revelation had a very prominent place in it. But the more I
studied it, the more confused I got, the more difficulties I
found. It did not get me through very far to glory. But then the
Lord gave me a clue, and showed me the spiritual principles
lying behind the Book of the Revelation, and I was able to
apprehend that book in a spiritual way. I do not mean that I

spiritualized everything, but I was able to apprehend it in a spiritual way. The cloud was lifted and there was life.

Take this matter of the coming of the Lord; and, of course, that is the coming of the Lord in glory, when He shall come in the clouds of glory, when He shall come to be glorified in His saints—the coming in by the east of the glory of the Lord. Have you noticed that in any time in the dispensation, when spiritual people have been gathered together, and in their gathering together have been speaking or singing of the coming of the Lord, how spontaneously the glory rises and comes in? Have you noticed that? Now, I do not believe that is merely psychological, and I do not believe it is because we are all thinking of ourselves, and of how great a day it will be when we are delivered from all our bonds. I believe rather this rising of glory is in spite of a very great deal. We have lived long enough, most of us, to know many people who believed fervently and said with emphasis that the Lord was coming in their lifetime and they would be raptured, and they have been in their graves for years. That is enough to turn you away from the whole subject and say, We have heard that before! It is enough to put you among those scoffers of whom Peter writes, who say, "Where is the promise of his coming? for, from the day that the fathers fell asleep, all things continue as they were from the beginning of the creation" (2 Peter 3:4, A.S.V.).

You may take that attitude, if you like; but it is in spite of all that that, when you contemplate the coming of the Lord, something gets the better of your mentality, your arguments, and all that bad history, and you find the glory rising. It is so, in spite of it all. Why is it? It was so at the beginning of the Church dispensation, and it has been so in every age; yet the Holy Spirit knew at the beginning that the Lord's coming would not be for a couple of thousand years, at any rate. But nevertheless there has been this spontaneous breaking out of real joy and glory at any moment when spiritual people have been dwelling upon the coming of the Lord. Why is it?

Because the Holy Spirit does not live in time at all, He does not belong to time. The Holy Spirit is outside of time and He already has the end with Him and He is the Spirit of the end, and when we really get into the Spirit we are in the Holy Spirit's end. If we dwell in the mind—oh, this reasoning line of things!—out of the Spirit, there is no joy. But when we let go and we are in the Spirit, we find ourselves with the Holy Spirit right at the end. We are outside of time, we are in the glory already in foreshadowing. The Holy Spirit is timeless and you get outside of time and you have everything; you have your finality, your fulness. Thus when John was in the Spirit in the isle of Patmos, he got right through to the end of things very quickly, the thing which we in time have not reached yet. That is what I mean by apprehending this matter spiritually. Beware of apprehending prophecy as a mental thing. The Holy Spirit in you in a living way will bring you into the good of things. Thus by the Spirit to-day we should stand with the light of the glorious fulness of the day of the Lord. We should be here as a testimony, not to prophetic things, not to teaching or doctrine about the Second Advent and all the problems connected therewith, but to the spiritual meaning of that. What is it?

Why, that is the end to which God has been working right through the centuries, the one thing upon which His heart is set, in which He has His satisfaction, His glory, His praise, His fulness, and the Holy Spirit is always there to make good something of that when we dwell upon it. He is there to be to us "the earnest of our inheritance," and to make us know it is a matter of faith, after all.

We do not always feel the glory of the coming of the Lord, we are not always living in the bright shining of that day, but "faith is the substance of things hoped for, the [proving] of things not seen," and when we let go our arguments and get into the Spirit, that is, get really into fellowship with the Holy Spirit, the weight of those arguments disappears, all the seeming contradictions in history go out. The glory of the Lord comes in by the gate which is toward the east.

> Yet a very little while, he that cometh shall come,
> and shall not tarry. But my righteous one shall live
> by faith.

The Lord then strengthen our faith and keep our hearts in faith.

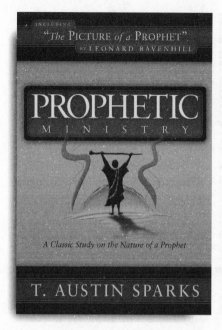

PROPHETIC MINISTRY
By T. Austin Sparks

What is God's purpose for His Church today? How can believers know and fulfill that purpose?

The Old Testament records God's desire for a people who would express His presence among the nations. He would be their King, in a Kingdom marked by spiritual vision and holy living. Prophets in that time constantly challenged the people toward these ideals, and warned of God's judgment when they disobeyed.

Then—good news! Through Jesus, God made His Kingdom available to everyone, regardless of age, background, race, or training. As each believer responds to the enlightening, cleansing, and purifying work of the Holy Spirit, the Church can once again proclaim God's presence among the nations of the world!

ISBN: 0-9677402-4-X

PILGRIM'S PROGRESS
By John Bunyan

John Bunyan's amazing *Pilgrim's Progress* is well into its fourth century of unparalleled popularity as the world's best-selling non-Biblical book in all history. Now in modern English comes *The New Amplified Pilgrim's Progress*. All of the age-old spiritual treasures are now carried to new heights of power and clarity in this new enhanced version. While this is perhaps the most adventure-filled and user-friendly adaptation ever penned, yet it is totally unabridged and, excepting certain amplified scenes, remains strictly faithful to Bunyan's original storyline.

Exciting new levels of love and joy, hope and humor are skillfully woven by master storyteller Jim Pappas, into this enchanting retelling of John Bunyan's immortal classic! Designed to return this spellbinding masterpiece of angels and giants, castles and dragon, to the fireside of the everyday reader.

ISBN: 0-7684-2051-2

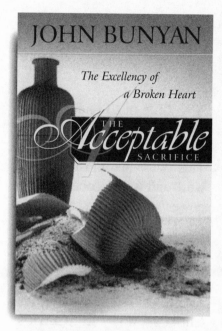

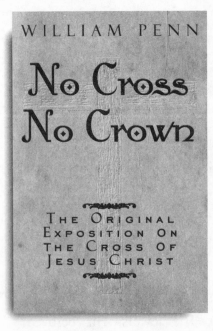

NO CROSS, NO CROWN
By William Penn

While in a London prison in 1668 William Penn wrote *No Cross, No Crown*. This was his most famous work and is a discourse on the power of the cross and self-denial. In dramatic and persuasive style Penn portrays the beauty and power of the cross as the only pathway to the crown. "Christ's cross, is Christ's way to Christ's crown." Penn's great passion was that this book would win the heart of man for his beloved Master.

ISBN: 0-9707919-1-7

Available at your local Christian bookstore.

Additional copies of this book and other
book titles from DESTINY IMAGE are
available at your local bookstore.

For a complete list of our titles,
visit us at www.destinyimage.com
Send a request for a catalog to:

Destiny Image₍ₐ₎ Publishers, Inc.

P.O. Box 310
Shippensburg, PA 17257-0310

*"Speaking to the Purposes of God for This Generation and for
the Generations to Come"*